3—

Columns

Tom Dryden

Columns

The Best of Doubting Thomas

Thomas Dryden

Library of Congress Number: 2001118521
ISBN #: Hardcover 1-4010-2844-6
Softcover 1-4010-2843-8

This book was printed in the United States of America.

To order additional copies of this book, contact:
Xlibris Corporation
1-888-7-XLIBRIS
www.Xlibris.com
Orders@Xlibris.com

Contents

537-DRYD

TO BERG

Acknowledgments

You wouldn't be holding this book in your hands if it weren't for the following:

- Phil Soto-Ortiz and Carolyn Ryzewicz of the *Wilton Villager*, who let me write 1,000 words (and sometimes more) in every issue.

- *Wilton Villager* readers, whose support and kind words inspire me to keep writing.

- Major John Gover, who taught English Literature my senior year at Wentworth Military Academy in Lexington, Missouri. He took the time to tell me I was a good writer and ought to consider becoming one professionally. So I did. Wherever you are, I salute you.

- Michael Noome, the most talented artist I know, whose work appears on the cover.

- My brother, Jerry, for leaving Auxvasse, Mo., as soon as he was able, so I knew that someday I could, too. Thanks for opening the window for me.

- My sister, Judy, for bringing home from college in the early 1960s the Tom Lehrer records I listened to for hours on end.

- My mother, Ruby who, at 88, is sharper than she was at my age. You're an inspiration to your children, grandchildren and great grandchildren.

- My late father, Bud, who taught me at an early age that if you want to do something right, you have to do it yourself.

- My teenage sons, Ben and Stuart, who keep me thinking young and feeling old.

- My wife, Judy, who reads every column before I submit it, and has wisely prevented me from printing things for which I would probably be lynched.

Introduction

When I was a growing up in Auxvasse, Mo. (population 808), two drunks—Sleepy Green and Cash Woods—got into a fight in the alley behind my father's general store. Sleepy slit Cash's throat. The next morning my dad appeared before the local judge to bail Sleepy out of jail.

"Mr. Dryden," the judge said, "You're a respected businessman. Why do you want to bail this no good son-of-a-bitch out of jail?"

"Because," my father replied calmly, "I've been wanting to slit Cash Woods' throat for 25 years."

Like my father, I, too, harbored an unspoken desire for 25 years: To become a columnist.

I majored in journalism in college. But I couldn't find a newspaper job when I graduated in 1973, so I became an advertising copywriter instead, working for a series of agencies before I started my own in 1989. Over the years, I've created advertising and what you probably call "junk mail"—I call it "bread and butter"—for some of the world's best-known brands. It's fun. It pays well.

But, deep-down, I always wanted to write for a newspaper. Specifically, to write a column for a newspaper.

I got my wish when, in September 1999, the *Wilton Villager*, a weekly in the small Connecticut town 50 miles north of New York where I have lived since 1985, ran an ad for a columnist. My wife pointed out the ad and, to her horror, I immediately sat down and wrote a letter explaining why I was the man for the job.

I was hired for $75 a week—money I use to treat her to dinner at a local restaurant every Friday night (tax, tip and wine excluded). But, truth be told, I'd write my column, *Doubting Thomas,* for free. I find it cathartic, after 27 years of writing copy for clients' products and services, to be able to write exactly what I want.

The ad said the *Villager* was looking for a columnist to "chime in" about local events. But I quickly ran out of chimes to ring.

Wilton is a beautiful New England town. Ancient stone walls separate two-acre plots of land on which stand huge homes. Most Wiltonites seem to have plenty of money to spend on imported SUVs and exotic vacations. I don't know a single soul who mows his own yard or cleans her own house. Each fall, a group of African-American students are imported into town, so Wilton children can someday say they went to school with kids who were different from them.

As subject matter for a column, however, the town is about as spicy as baked cod served with sides of mashed potatoes and cauliflower. Wilton residents, who spend their days making decisions in executive suites or shuttling kids from soccer to lacrosse practices, want nothing more than to be left alone. They seem to believe that, as Robert Frost wrote about another part of New England, "good fences good neighbors make" and guard their privacy zealously. Unlike my small Missouri hometown where everyone knew everyone else's business, Wilton is the kind of place where families can live next door to each other for 10 years and never see the inside of each other's stretch-colonials.

The only interest most Wiltonites share is the public school system, acclaimed as one of the country's best. But I wasn't about to write columns about the schools, since my kids attend them.

So, after my first few columns in which I wrote about the

heavy traffic on Route 7, a road the town has prevented from being improved for 40 years, and the lack of any organized activities for men in Wilton, I began digressing from the column's original purpose. I wrote about politics, television, travel and health. About being a 25-year-old trapped in an aging boomer body. About my teenage sons. My dogs. My wife and the bed in which we sleep (she likes the mattress firm, I like it marshmallow-soft). I wrote about conversations overheard on airplanes, behavior observed in bookstores and other oddities of life in a world in which common courtesy and common sense often seem to have taken flight.

Even though I was off-strategy, the people at the *Wilton Villager* never said a word because *Doubting Thomas* was an immediate hit. I try to make most of my columns humorous. As the youngest child in my family, I learned early that I had to make people laugh if I wanted to get noticed, so wry observations come easily to me. But every so often I like to come out of left field with a serious column, to keep readers on their toes, and to prove to myself that I can write them.

I hope to continue writing *Doubting Thomas* for years to come. (Actually, I'm hoping this book will enable me to be discovered by a newspaper syndicate so I can write columns full-time, be invited to give commencement speeches at colleges and travel around the country plugging books for which I'll earn millions in royalties. I know, however, that the odds of a 49-year-old small-town columnist being "discovered" are about as slim as a 101-year-old cross-eyed divorcee finding true love.)

Whether or not this book earns me fame and fortune, I hope you'll enjoy reading this collection of some of my favorite columns as much as I've enjoyed writing them.

Having the *Times* of our lives

Did you catch the cover story in *The New York Times* magazine last Sunday entitled, "How The New Suburban Majority Is Changing America?"

If so, I hope you laughed yourself as silly as I did. It was hilarious, though I doubt the reporters and editors who contributed to it intended for it to be that way.

The entire issue was devoted to life in the suburbs. Readers learned that the real power and culture in America now emanates from the 'burbs to the cities rather than the other way around.

This late-breaking news was reported in classic overwrought *Times* fashion by reporters who *actually left New York* in search of the real world and were astounded to find there is, indeed, life in the 'burbs, though the reporters pointedly refrained from classifying it as intelligent life.

Don't get me wrong. To me, New York is the most exciting place in America, perhaps on earth. I lived there for five years in my late 20s and early 30s and if we hadn't been seized by an irrational desire to procreate, we'd be there still. I love everything about New York. Well, almost everything.

But even when I lived in New York—and especially now that I don't—I found the *Times'* myopic view of the world maddeningly parochial. It's clear to me that many of its reporters and editors have never willingly set foot outside Manhattan, and have no clue that the majority of Americans doesn't see things the way *The New York Times* editorial board does.

The "suburban" issue of the magazine was a prime example. Those brave reporters who ventured out of the city to report on life in the 'burbs reported back with the same wide-eyed wonder one would have expected from the first reporters admitted to Albania, a country that had been virtually shut off from the rest of the world, after the fall of Communism.

They seemed astonished, for example, to learn suburbanites are buying small houses on prime lots and tearing them down to build large new ones—even though people in New York have been doing that since the 1600s.

Richard Rayner contributed "Back In The Swing," an article about a trend he has been assured is now commonplace in Orange County, California. It's something I'm confident will arrive in Wilton soon: wife-swapping parties.

"I catch sight of a woman dancing naked in front of a barbecue fire. Almost as if a switch had been thrown, inhibitions evaporate and the scene, in its co-mingling of the sexual and the prosaic, becomes surreal, the suburbs, as they might be perceived through the lens of a David Lynch . . . In spite of my empathy for these people, I am repulsed."

Darn, I was gonna rent out the Old Town Hall and invite all my readers for a swinging evening some Saturday soon. But if anyone's going to be repulsed, well forget about it.

Food editor Molly O'Neill reported that in the 'burbs, Sunday brunch is considered "a great opportunity to show off the cut of the lawn, the new wallpaper or the gleam of the expensive copper gourmet tools in the kitchen" and provided recipes for Bloody Marys and Eggs Benedict. "In the suburbs," O'Neill wrote, "brunch rules." As if she's ever been to one in any 'burb that didn't end with "Hampton."

Amy Bloom, a *Times* correspondent who moved to Durham,

Connecticut, a few years ago, reported that the town is "much more white than I like and much more Christian." I wonder what she expected.

The *Times* reported that today's "monster garages are receptacles for a whole slew of suburban status symbols" and have "all the amenities of home." Common amenities apparently include a $4,000 Bang & Olufsen sound system, $3,800 Muller refrigerator available in 200 colors, and a $3,700 Viking Gas Grill. (Maybe we'll have that wife-swapping party in the garage of some Wiltonite who has all these toys. Anyone wanna host?)

But my favorite article was contributed by our Westport neighbor, Martha Stewart, who informed *Times* readers why, after 25 years, she's leaving town.

Martha cries that chain stores have moved into downtown, squeezing out locally-owned businesses, making Westport like so many other "shopping destination towns." (Hey Martha, ever heard of Kmart? You know, the chain store you do commercials for, hawking your paint, sheets and all that other stuff you put your name on? How many hundreds of thousands of small businesses has Kmart helped destroy?)

Martha laments that all the garden tours and Westport Historical Society functions she has hosted lately "have not garnered me any new local friendships—nor dinner invitations."

Let's be real here. Who wouldn't be intimidated to ask Martha Stewart, the world's most perfect cook and hostess, to dinner? ("Hi Martha, Tom here, calling to invite you over tonight. No, nothing fancy—we're throwing some hot dogs on the Jenn-Air. And Martha, would you mind stopping by Hayday and picking up some sausage casings and equal parts of coarsely ground veal, beef and pork along with some coriander, basil and thyme, so we can make them up nice and fresh the way you like them?")

Here's an idea. If the *Times* wants to see what life is like in a real suburb, let's invite its reporters and editors here to Wilton for a picnic. (We'll ask Martha, too.)

We can hold it at Merwin Meadows. We'll wear black to make

our guests feel at home, and make sure we have plenty of non-whites and non-Christians on hand (even if we have to borrow some) so everyone will feel comfortable.

After the meal, we can crank up the Bang & Olafsen from someone's garage, get naked and have sex with each others' spouses under the pavilion. (I know who I want to see dancing naked by the barbecue.)

Let's show those New Yorkers once and for all why we're so glad we live here in the quintessential suburb, Wilton USA.

Hey baby, I'm your handy man

I'm the least handy person on the face of the planet. I don't understand how things go together, stay together, what makes them work. Never have, never will and I'll never stop trying, despite my wife's pleas.

I think my penchant for fixing things is a competitive response to my brother who, naturally, was born with a pipe wrench in his left hand, a hammer in his right. (My mother says it was a difficult delivery.)

This is a man who, in one afternoon, installed a skylight in his kitchen and in a week built a billiards room in his basement whereas I can't hang a picture without causing sparks to fly because I hit a live wire.

As I write this, I have a knot the size of an orange on top of my head because last night I tried to change the battery in our downstairs smoke detector.

It took just a moment to remove the cover and the old battery, and to snap the new one into position.

But replacing the cover was torture. Try as I might, it kept crashing to the floor because I couldn't get it to fit back into the plastic housing. When I finally did get the cover to stay (by duct-taping it to the ceiling) and pushed the "test" button, it was clear the battery wasn't connecting.

When I removed the cover, the battery shot out of the clips at 100 mph and smacked me upside the head, knocking me off the ottoman I was standing on and into the wall, creating an elbow-sized crater. If our house goes up in flames with my family in it, I hope the readers of this column will sue First Alert on behalf of our estate for making a product one needs an MIT degree to maintain.

Plumbing is another challenge. Every so often, our toilets start making whirring sounds that my wife tells me means our well could run dry. We wait until all the toilets are making this sound then call a plumber who comes in . . . replaces parts . . . and charges us an arm and a leg.

One Saturday morning when my wife was out, I heard the toilet in our bathroom start whirring. I decided I could fix it and save a few bucks.

Naturally, this isn't a standard white toilet, but one of those squatty, vaguely French-looking bidet-like contraptions I've personally never felt comfortable using because, when I sit on it, my knees are higher than my face.

I went to the hardware store and bought a kit containing one of those plastic round ball thingies. I took out the old ball thingie and the lever to which it was attached, and replaced it with the new one. But when I was finished, it didn't work. So I went back and bought a different kit.

When my wife came home and saw plumbing parts spread across two rooms, she was as horrified as if she had come home to find me performing a heart transplant on one of the dogs.

After six or seven hours (and three more trips to the store), I was satisfied I had solved the problem. That evening, as I was sitting in the living room, I looked up and saw a huge stain spreading across the ceiling. I'd pulled the toilet from the pipes, which were leaking.

It cost more than a thousand dollars to repair the ceiling and, to add insult to injury, the toilet still whirs.

Electricity is a particular specialty. Once before a dinner

party, I replaced a chandelier that, ten minutes before guests were to arrive, crashed down onto the table set with good china, smashing it to smithereens. Another time I installed a dimmer that caught fire.

When Santa brought our kids a Nintendo one year, I spent all day Christmas trying to connect it to the TV through a maze of cable and VCR wires. By the time I was finished, the TV didn't work. I finally had to pay the cable company to come and put it together.

The highlight of my Mr. Fix-It career came several years ago when I decided to replace two steps on our deck that had rotted. I bought some boards and a circular saw to cut them.

As I was merrily buzzing through the first board, the saw's blade suddenly stopped. I thought I must have unplugged it, but when I checked the socket, it was still plugged in.

I called the Black & Decker hotline but the person on the other end might as well have been speaking Cantonese for all I understood.

My son finally pointed out that I had sawed through the power cord. So I went out and bought another saw. (Someone later told me I could have bought a new cord but how the hell would I have known that?)

The first time I stepped on the top stair I had installed, it snapped in two.

This column is being written in longhand because last weekend I took my home PC apart to install a new memory chip and video card so I could enjoy better graphics when playing my favorite computer game, Flight Simulator. I had three screws left over when I was done and, needless to say, the computer won't even turn on.

My brother visits every year, brings his tool box and graciously spends a day of his vacation fixing things. I always leave the house (because I'm jealous and feeling inadequate) and my wife stays home with him and points out things that need fixing.

Once, after he had spent the day planing doors that wouldn't shut, changing locks that wouldn't lock and replacing fuses to outlets that wouldn't work, he and my wife were in the kitchen (undoubtedly saying bad things about me).

"Is there anything else you need fixed?" he asked. "I can't think of it," she said.

At that moment, the new telephone I had installed the month before rang, fell off the wall and onto the floor, as it did every time someone called. We had become used to it.

"Oh yeah," she told him, "Would you mind fixing that, too?"

Hate telemarketers? Join the chorus.

I have pet peeves galore.

Dimwits who drive down the highway with their turn signals blinking blinking blinking for five miles.

Gas-guzzling, view-blocking SUVs the size of house trailers.

The dancing paper clip that appears on my computer screen every time I type the word "dear" which asks, *"It looks like you're writing a letter, would you like help?" (I'm a writer, you're a paper clip, the only way you can help me is if whoever at Microsoft invented you swallows you and chokes to death.)*

But nothing—nothing—sends me to the moon like telemarketers who interrupt me in the privacy of my home evenings and weekends hawking heating oil, credit cards, vinyl siding, investments, insurance, you name it.

I'm in advertising. More specifically, direct marketing, which you probably call "junk mail." You may find junk mail annoying as it piles up on the floor of your spiffy new SUV or on the kitchen counter, but hey, at least I've never broken into your house and assaulted you while you were eating dinner, in the shower or making whoopee. But it happens thousands of times every day right here in 06897 where, as a demographically-desirable affluent zip code, we are considered prime pickings by telemarketers.

My wife gets calls from her girlfriends almost hourly, and my teenage son can easily receive a dozen calls in one evening from his friends. I, on the other hand, hardly ever get calls at home. I suspect most of you guys don't. So when I do, it's almost a sure bet it's a telemarketer.

Whenever I pick up the phone and hear a voice, *"May I speak to Thomas Dryden please?"* my blood pressure skyrockets because nobody I know calls me Thomas.

"He just passed away and we have to leave for the funeral," I'll say.

"I've heard that one before Mr. Dryden," they'll reply, launching into their canned spiel

Or I try another approach. *"He's in Los Angeles being arraigned for the murder of Nicole Brown Simpson."*

"*I see,*" the voice will say, "*And when will he be back?*"

People representing "investment" firms I've never heard of—invariably named Vinny—are the wiliest when it comes to getting through. My wife has told these callers I'm being held hostage by Colombian terrorists, only to have them call back two minutes later, hoping I'll pick up the phone.

One—to whom I have to give credit—told my son he was an old school pal of mine, so my son called me to the phone.

"Thomas, this is Vinny of Scuzbucket Securities."

"You say we went to school together."

"We did, don't you remember?"

"Where'd we go?"

"Uh...Harvard?"

Click.

Once I received a call from American Express saying they noticed I had children and, if one was college-age, would I like a credit card issued in that child's name?

"Yes," I answered.

"And what is your child's name?"

"Clyde."

"And what is Clyde's Social Security number?"

"I don't know, his card's in the safe deposit box at the bank."

"That's OK, we can use yours."

Our dachshund, Clyde, now possesses an Optima card that earns him Delta Skymiles whenever he presents it worldwide. Unfortunately, he wears an invisible fence collar so he doesn't get many opportunities to shop or travel.

I've tried everything to make sure they never call back. I've acted like I'm happy to hear from them. *"Oh man, thanks for calling, it's so lonely being confined here in this house wearing an ankle bracelet with nobody but Regis and Kathie Lee to talk to, so what's the weather like where you are?"*

I've acted crazy. *"Hello Mr. Dryden, I'm calling tonight to ask which one of our three brochures you'd like me to send you—vinyl siding, windows or insulation?"*

"I want the red one."

"But Mr. Dryden, none of them are red. One's blue, one's orange, one's purple."

"I only read brochures with red covers."

A few months ago, I tried something new. And guess what, folks? It *works!*

I want to share my strategy with you in the hopes that every household in Wilton will follow my example. If we do, I'm convinced word will get out in telemarketing circles to avoid 06897 like the plague.

The secret is . . . don't talk to them when they call. *Sing* to them.

That's right, as they're announcing their name and the company they're representing, break into song—the first song that pops into your mind. I've sang "Last Kiss" to First Union . . ."Livin' La Vida Loca" to Sprint . . . "Jesus Loves Me" to Prodigy . . . and last night I broke into "Having My Baby" for someone who said he was calling me at the personal request of Pat Buchanan. *"Deep inside you, my seed is growing . . . my seed inside you's growing, aren't you happy knowing . . . that you're having my ba-by."*

He called his co-workers over. *"Hey listen to this guy, he's singing. That's a new one."* He put me on speakerphone and he and his co-telemarketers laughed nervously, before they finally hung up.

But most hang up immediately. More important, they don't call back. I can almost hear the pencil scratching my name and number off their list over the dead phone line.

So c'mon Wilton, why not give it a go? You have nothing to lose—it's not like you're going to run into these callers at Keeler's Hardware, who'll point to you and yell, "*He's/she's a psycho!*"

And who knows? You, your family and all of your neighbors here in 06897 might—just might—be able to enjoy some peace and quiet for a change.

Sunday at the bookstore

I drive to a neighboring town every Sunday to one of those super bookstores that are roughly the size of football fields.

I tell you this not to impress you with any intellectual bent on my part. I write advertising for a living, remember, so I'm no rocket scientist.

It's just that I like to see what new title Stephen King has managed to bang out since the previous weekend, and to spend an hour or so surreptitiously reading magazines that, were I to subscribe to them, would wind up under the bed along with dozens of others I hope to get around to someday, like the June 11, 1992 "What To Do This Summer" issue of *New York* magazine.

My visit always begins with a stop at the store's coffee bar. I order a double espresso in a paper cup, so I can browse the aisles while getting stoned on caffeine.

Last Sunday, as usual, I walked into the store and immediately headed for the coffee bar. In front of the counter stood a woman about my age, placing her order. Dressed in a black turtleneck, her hair was pulled back into a tight bun like Lilith, Frasier's wife on *Cheers*. She was wearing a pair of those retro Batgirl-like glasses some women wear so people will be so taken aback by the ugliness of the spectacles that they overlook the plainness of their faces.

"I want a decaf cappuccino made with skim milk," she said.

The man behind the counter went to work twisting knobs that released flatulent-sounding hisses and, a minute later, presented her order in a standard-issue brown paper cup.

"I want that in a mug, I'll drink it here," she said, indicating the small seating area containing tables and chairs behind her.

He carefully transferred her coffee into a porcelain mug, leaving a half-inch gap between the liquid and the brim.

"Fill it all the way to the top," she ordered, sounding like Leona Helmsley, and without apologizing for her failure to specify a mug in the first place.

He went back to work twisting knobs and, in 30 seconds or so, placed a steaming mug, filled to the top, on the counter before her.

By now, three or four people had formed a line behind me.

"That'll be $2.39," the man behind the counter said.

"I want a chocolate biscotti with that," she said, pointing to a glass case in which three rows of rectangular cookies were displayed. "Gimme one from the center row."

He reached into the case with tongs, picked out a biscotti and placed it on a plate, which he set on the counter next to her coffee.

She leaned down to inspect it.

"That one has icing, I don't want icing," she informed him, as if he should have known she had an deathly aversion to icing when she ordered her cappuccino with skim milk. "What are the other two?"

"The left row is plain chocolate, the right row is chocolate with almonds."

She bent down in front of the front of the case, as if selecting a diamond she would be wearing forever, and thought hard for several moments, during which time several more people joined the line.

"I'll have one of those," she said, indicating the chocolate with almond row.

With his tongs, the man placed the frosted biscotti back in the center row, removed a cookie from the right row, and replaced it on the plate, which he set in front of her.

"No, not *that* one, I want the one at the front of the case," she said with contempt, as if she had caught him stealing from her. "It's bigger."

The man patiently exchanged the cookies, taking care not to crumble the biscotti from the front of the row as he placed it on the plate.

"Will that be all?" he asked, pushing the plate toward her.

She looked down at the plate in horror as if there were a cockroach crawling across it. "That one has nuts, I can't digest nuts. Give me one of those," she said, pointing to the row of plain chocolate biscotti.

I could restrain myself no longer. "I can only imagine the hell you must put real estate agents and car dealers through," I told her, as the man once again transferred cookies from the plate to the display case and back to the plate. She turned to glare at me. The man caught my eye but said nothing. His expression seemed to say, "This is nothing unusual buddy."

"That'll be $3.59," he said.

I fully expected her to demand a fresh cappuccino since hers was cold by now, but, to my relief, she opened her purse.

She dug through the duffel bag-sized purse tentatively for a few moments, and then, with more urgency, digging the same way my beagle digs for moles in the back yard. She placed the purse on the counter and began removing items from it. A small package of Kleenex, sunglasses, an address book, cell phone, keys, a handful of pennies and nickels and a package of Trident appeared as she continued her search.

After a minute or so, it was apparent to all of us who had been waiting.

"I left my billfold at home," she told the man behind the

counter, who looked at me as if pleading with me to pay for this woman's order, so he could get on with his job.

And I suppose I could have.

But I didn't.

My little black friend from Aruba

Ocean was a black, 15-pound mongrel with tarter-caked teeth, sour breath and cataract–glazed eyes that appeared green in every single photograph we ever took. We were crazy about him.

Five years ago, en route to a vacation in Aruba, I promised my 8-year-old I'd get him a present if he could last the week without provoking a fight with his brother. "I want another dog," he replied. We laughed. Our family already had two, so a third dog was out of the question. Besides, it seemed like a safe bet.

An hour after we arrived, I spotted the little black dog, strutting purposefully along the beach, his head held high as if he were on a mission. He was.

He stopped at the Hyatt Beach Bar, where the bartender served him a bowl of water he lapped up gratefully. He then proceeded up and down the beach, begging sun-bathers for food. Few could resist sharing their potato chips with him. Potato chips remained his favorite snack until the very end.

I've fallen in love on-the-spot twice. On the day I met my wife. And for the second time on that palm-spotted beach, where, in the distance, calypso music was playing.

Reading my mind, my wife had five words to say. "Don't even think about it."

I observed him for most of the week. His poor-little-beggar-dog routine never varied. At night, we would find him curled up under a bush, where he was safest from iguanas which, in Aruba, are the size of small alligators.

I asked lifeguards and vendors who worked on the beach if he belonged to anyone. All agreed he didn't and that he was a nuisance.

One morning, I went to the beach alone and plopped down in a chaise. The little black dog came up to me. I talked to him. He seemed to understand. *"Little black dog, I'm going to walk back to the hotel. Follow me, and I'll take it as a sign you will consider becoming a part of my family . . . and you will become a prince among dogs."*

I walked a hundred yards without looking back, hoping he was following. He was.

I stopped. He stopped. I walked a hundred more. So did he. Our eyes met. His seemed to say, *"I trust you, mon. "*

I threw a towel over him, and smuggled him through the lobby, up to our room.

His ribs protruded. He was covered with fleas. One eye was swollen shut with infection. I took him to a vet I found in the phone book and instructed him to give the dog the shots needed to get through U.S. Customs. The vet wrote "Lucky" under "name" on the dog's inoculation record, but the boys named him "Ocean."

Ocean flew with us to America, and was driven to his new home in Connecticut, a big white colonial surrounded by green grass on which he promptly relieved himself, marking it "mine."

He was housebroken instantly. And, while I'm the one who wanted him, he immediately became my wife's shadow, not mine. He followed her everywhere—even to the bathroom.

Our other dogs would invite him to join them in play. He would stare back blankly. Perhaps he never understood the language American dogs speak. In any case, play was a foreign concept to someone who had spent his entire life foraging for food and outrunning iguanas.

Twice a day, when his bowl was filled with Mighty Dog, he would break into a joyful dance and bark, as if declaring, *"Hey mon, what a great country! I don't have to beg no more."*

And, despite the fact that he was accustomed to the tropics, he loved to stay inside, in the air-conditioning. We'd let him out to hike his leg, and within a few seconds he'd be back at the door, as if afraid the house would vanish while he was away from it, along with his new-found good fortune.

Already grey-muzzled when we found him, Ocean grew greyer through the late 90s. About a year ago, he found the stairs impossible to negotiate, so we started carrying him up and down.

One day this summer, I detected a lump in his chest. We rushed him to the vet who said it appeared to be an allergic reaction. But after several months of expensive treatments, as he became thinner and less steady on his feet, it was clear Ocean's days were numbered.

The end came suddenly. We were planning to leave the next day for a long weekend. That morning, the vet suggested that Ocean should spend the weekend in the hospital for observation, rather than check into the kennel with our other dogs. We agreed to bring him back in the morning.

Ocean hated to be boarded, to be separated from us. He knew he was mortally ill. So he decided he would rather die in his beloved home, surrounded by his family.

My wife says he danced and barked for his dinner, as usual, at 5, before she left to meet some friends.

When I arrived home at 7, he was curled up on his blanket, unable to raise his head or stand. He looked up at me as if to say, *"Sorry mon, there's nothing you can do about it."*

I petted him and, as his breathing became more labored, spoke gently, telling him to go ahead, to let go. I thanked him for the lessons he had taught us about trust, about gratitude, about not judging by outward appearances, about giving and receiving love with no-strings-attached. But he seemed to be waiting for something.

When he heard my wife's car turn into the driveway, he lifted his head. When she walked through the door, his ears perked up, and he seemed to relax. A few moments later, he crawled under our poster bed where he slept every night, fell on his side, breathed deeply three times, and was gone.

I like to think he's back in Aruba, but that Aruba has changed.

Palms still sway. In the distance, steel drums still pound out calypso. He still has the freedom to work the beach, begging potato chips from strangers.

But where the beach bar stood now stands a white air-conditioned colonial, surrounded by a carpet of green grass.

In the house lives a family who loves him, who defends him from iguanas, who keeps his bowl filled with fresh cool water and serves him Mighty Dog twice a day.

He knows he can come home whenever he wants, and he always does.

Yes, you can bring a bottle. Of Scope.

You're all invited to my house for a festive dinner party. It will be a meal you'll never forget.

I'm importing several of New York's hottest, hippest chefs right here to little old Wilton to work their culinary wizardry in my kitchen and you, my loyal readers, are the lucky beneficiaries of my largesse.

We'll start with your choice of two appetizers—"a pyramid of delectably earthy rich chicken liver mousse, slathered onto grilled country bread and draped with red onion compote," and "steak tartare with raw egg yolk and arugula."

What? You say you appreciate the invitation but you've got to be in Buffalo for a Hillary fundraiser that night?

Then I'll pull out all the stops and demand that the chefs prepare my favorite—citrus-cured sardines with "the unctuous texture of octopus jelled into a kind of headcheese."

That, I'm sure, is all you'll need to call Hillary's people and make your excuses.

I'm having trouble deciding which of three altogether different and equally tasty entrees to serve. Since you're my guest of honor, I'll let you decide.

Should it be "squab with foi-gras-porcine and pig's feet stuffing?"

"Meltingly rich beef cheeks with delicate chive spaetzle?"

Or perhaps I should play it safe and serve something less exotic, an old Dryden family favorite I'm sure you also enjoy in the privacy of your own home—"lamb brain ravioli."

By now, I'm sure you've lost the few extra pounds you packed on over the holidays.

So let's wipe up the floor and continue, shall we?

"Tom," you say. "I'd as soon eat algae from my septic tank with one of those wooden spoons that used to come with cups of Good Humor ice cream."

Well don't blame me if you're not sophisticated enough to recognize gourmet food.

Blame, instead, some of the leading New York food critics who, in recent months, have rhapsodized about the aforementioned dishes in publications you read on a regular basis.

I like to know what's going on in the world. So I read just about anything and everything I can get my hands on, including restaurant reviews in leading newspapers and magazines.

Don't get me wrong here. I appreciate it is the job of the food critic to identify new trends, urge chefs onward and upward to new culinary heights, and to make people like you and me feel like what we are—suburban yokels whose idea of dining out is the drive-through window of Boston Market.

While we're inching to the front of the line, 50 miles to the south gourmands wearing black are meeting in the bar areas of impossibly chic restaurants, air-kissing, being shown to their tables by the maitre d' and ordering . . . lamb brains?

I'll take a quarter roast chicken with sides of mashed potatoes, spinach and cornbread any day.

What on earth are these food critics thinking? That any reader in his or her right mind would willingly pay good money for dishes concocted from body parts Purina sent back?

Years ago, when I first started my own agency, I landed a job producing a guide to Morocco for Royal Air Maroc. (I'd never been there at the time but hey, I could imagine.) The folks at the Moroccan Consulate gave me a cookbook I still have, so I could describe typical Moroccan cuisine.

On page 102 is a recipe for Steamed Sheep's Head. The recipe advises cooks to, "Ask the butcher to chop off the horns. Take out the brains and shake the head hard to make sure any maggots that might be tucked away inside the ears and mouth fall out."

Needless to say, that recipe didn't make it into my final draft.

But guess what? A reviewer for *New York* magazine recently went into ecstasy over a restaurant's "silky calf's head with pumpkin seed oil." M-m-m-m, good.

The dishes these reviewers order are revolting enough. Worse yet, they usually demand that the kitchen prepare their orders to their own Jeffrey Dahmer-like tastes, then criticize the chef if he fails to serve it that way.

One reviewer wrote that she specifies "liver, quiveringly rare." Now that's a word picture for you.

There's something I've always wondered about that I have to lay on the table (so to speak). Restaurant reviewers almost always take guests with them, so they can sample not only their own entrée but whatever their guests order.

If you dine with a critic who orders lamb brain ravioli or calf's head, do you offer that critic a good-night kiss? And if so, do you slip the critic a little tongue (rare of course)?

Not on your life.

P&G doesn't make enough Scope for that.

Call me a fuddy-duddy, but I have to think these reviewers are pulling our collective leg (of lamb, served deliciously rare with a sauce of goat cheese, chervil and balsamic vinegar). I imagine they write their reviews . . . submit them . . . then wait to see if their editors will slip them in during a particularly hectic news day when they don't have time to read them carefully.

And when they see their reviews in print, they hoot about it with their friends as they sit down to plates of pasta in their favorite bistros.

But maybe I'm wrong. So I'm planning this swell dinner party. And I invite you to join me.

If you don't like the food, you can always have Kraft Macaroni & Cheese with my 13-year-old and nurse a glass of wine.

I'm planning to serve a California Merlot I read about, a wine that has a "nice friendly nose with some tobacco and tar. Very young, but with some guts."

Regrets only.

Fandango time at the Meadowlands

11:30 p.m. Monday, October 23.

I'm writing this on a napkin at the Sports Bar of the Meadowlands Sheraton in New Jersey where, three blocks away, my 17-year-old and three buddies are attending the pivotal Jets/Miami Dolphins game. They lucked into tickets. I volunteered to drive them. Actually, I insisted and said I'd wait at the Sheraton. Despite the God-awful music blaring from the CD player all the way from Wilton, they're good kids and I enjoyed their all-over-the-place conversation.

When I arrived three hours ago, a cocktail party was going on in the lobby. Some company holding its international sales meeting. Banners were suspended from the ceiling with motivational propaganda—slogans like "Pulling Together." There were probably 200 sales types, mostly foreigners. You can always tell foreigners by their weird-looking shoes.

The party ended an hour ago. Most of the salespeople have wandered in here. On the jukebox Eric Clapton is blaring at approximately 1,000 decibels. *"You got me on my knees, Layla . . ."*

Directly in front of my corner table is a couple playing fooseball. Click. Click. Click. Click. All other eyes are glued to the five TV screens hanging from the ceiling. Not that anyone can hear a word the announcers are saying. The music is loud. VERY LOUD.

It's the third quarter. The Jets are behind big-time. I'm drinking coffee. My third cup. I want a drink, but that would defeat the purpose of me chauffeuring.

Barbra Streisand and Donna Summer's disco hit, "Enough is Enough," is blasting from the jukebox. If, when I die, I go to hell, I'll be sentenced to hearing it forever, an endless loop of *"I can't go on, I can't go on no more."* The plate-glass window behind me is rattling.

I brought a book I picked up at the library used-book sale, *The Memoirs of Richard Nixon.* I'm halfway through this bizarre man's 1,100-page life story. The first vote I ever cast in 1972 I cast against him, and I was glad to see him go when he resigned. Nevertheless, he's always fascinated me. Two years ago I visited his presidential library in California. Someone had rented out the garden for a Bar Mitzvah. People were dancing the Hava Nagilah not 10 feet from Dick and Pat's graves.

At the table next to me a salesman from Canada has spent the last hour trying to pick up a British saleswoman who looks vaguely like Princess Di if you've knocked back enough Bass Ales, which he has. I can tell he's Canadian because he says "a-boat" for "about." I was thinking he was a-boat to get the nod to go upstairs to her room, until a Frenchman with nerd glasses pulled up a chair. Probably one of their supervisors, so they can't tell him to buzz off.

A country song comes on. *"Hey pretty lady can't you give me a sign? I'd give you anything to make you mine all mine."*

Midnight. Fourth quarter. The Jets are down 30-7. My son

and I both have cell phones. I'm hoping he'll call, telling me he and his friends are on their way, knowing it's hopeless. Fat chance.

This is surreal. A nun—*a nun*—just walked in, and has bellied up to the U-shaped bar, where she's talking with a group of cigar-smoking men. Wait a minute. It's almost Halloween. Maybe she's dressed up as a nun. But she looks my age. I don't think women in their late 40s dress up like nuns and hang around sports bars. Now she's looking at the screen and cheering. 7:27 left. Dolphins 30, Jets 20. It's 12:20 a.m.

Madonna's "La Isla Bonita" is on the jukebox. My coffee cup is vibrating. What's with Madonna popping out all those babies anyway, kids she saddles with names like Lourdes and Rocco, as if they're not going to have enough problems in their lifetimes with her as their mother?

With five minutes left, it's the Fins 30, Jets 23. The crowd is nuts. Beyond nuts.

A table of chain-smoking Japanese men who weren't even feigning interest in the game have turned around and are watching the TV. Some of the American salesmen are trying to explain football to them, but you can tell by the glazed look on their faces they don't get it.

With 3:33 left, the Jets score again. Tie game.

People are cheering. A man at the bar with 10 empty longnecks in front him is yelling over and over, "Who Let the Dogs Out? J-E-T-S!" Nobody pays him any attention.

On the jukebox, Freddie Mercury is wailing, *"I see a little silhouetto of a man. Scaramouche, scaramouche, will you do the fandango?"*

Miami scores. 37-30.

The French nerd knocks his Amstel Light over, drenching Di's white sweater. She jumps up, and runs out. Looking disgusted, the Canadian goes to the bar, orders another Bass Ale and starts watching the game.

At 12:55 a.m. with 42 seconds to go, the Jets tie it up again.

Sudden Death. The Jets have earned it. What are the odds of a team scoring 30 points in one quarter?

Gloria Estefan is on the jukebox now. *"Cause tonight we're . . . gonna party, 'til we see the break of day."*

Another coffee please. Yes, I know I'll never get to sleep.

The man yelling "Who Let The Dogs Out" falls off his stool.

Di returns in jeans, and the Canadian's face lights up like a Christmas tree. Fandango time.

At 1:25, the Jets score, and, as sudden as death, it's over.

My phone rings. "Dad? Was there a TV in the bar?"

"Yes," I answer.

"Unbelievable, wasn't it?"

He's bursting with the exuberance of a 17-year-old who has just eyewitnessed the greatest comeback in NFL history, on a school night no less.

And, for one all-too-brief moment, despite the late hour, I feel 17, too.

"See you in 10, " he says, disconnecting the phone.

"I'll be waiting out front," I tell the receiver.

Lessons my mothers taught me

I am the product of many mothers.

My biological mother to this day introduces me as her "baby" and apologizes for not having breast-fed me, as she did my older siblings. For some reason, breast-feeding was important to the women in her family.

Her own grandmother, who had 17 children, was so enamored of breast-feeding that she continued to nurse her youngest child, Luther, long past the time she should have stopped. When Luther was six, the sheriff showed up to inquire why the child wasn't at school, and found him being breast-fed on the front porch, both of his feet planted firmly on the floor, as his mother rocked back and forth in a chair smoking a corncob pipe. "He ain't old enough," his mother informed the sheriff.

From my mother, I learned to love reading, travel, and to how to make perfect angel food cakes. (Buy a Duncan Hines mix.)

Then there were my TV mothers—mothers with sons roughly my age—on the shows I watched faithfully. Growing up with my nose pressed to the boob tube, I learned almost as much—maybe more—from those mothers as I did my own.

One of my favorites was Timmy's mom, played by June Lockhart, on *Lassie*, which I watched every Sunday night during the late 50s.

Timmy's mother, Ruth, lived on a desert ranch with her husband, son, and, of course, Lassie, who was smarter than all of them rolled together. Timmy's mother always wore spike heels.

As a child, I wondered why Ruth would allow Timmy to be raised in such a godforsaken place, which had tumbleweeds everywhere, abandoned wells to fall into, wild cougars, etc.

As an adult, I think I've figured it out. She had kidnapped Timmy from his real parents, and was hiding out where nobody could find them.

Ruth gave Timmy carte blanche to explore the canyons and rattlesnake-infested gullies of the area, secure in the knowledge that if he needed help, Lassie would sound the alarm. That's a far cry from today's neurotic mothers who insist their children carry pagers or cell phones everywhere they go. *"Oops gotta go, just got a page from Timmy. Looks like he's fallen in a well again."*

From Ruth, I learned that good mothers give their children rope with plenty of slack to explore the world, and let them figure out for themselves how to get out of any wells into which they fall.

Her suburban counterpart was June Cleaver, mother of Beaver and Wally on *Leave It To Beaver*. June, too, always wore heels, but never left her kitchen. However, unlike Ruth, June was overly protective of her children and smothered them with so many questions after school as they ate her freshly-baked cookies that you just knew they must hate her, and would never visit once they left the nest.

Mrs. Cleaver couldn't cope with her boys, and would wait until her husband, Ward, came home so he could deal with their troubled, dim-witted son, Beaver. "Ward, something's bothering the Beaver." I suspect that while Ward talked it over with Beav, June went to the kitchen and drank directly from a bottle of Smirnoff to dull the pain she must have felt from wearing heels all day on a linoleum floor, not to mention having given birth to a loser like Beaver.

From June, I learned that a mother—even one who makes cookies from scratch instead of buying Nabisco—shouldn't be afraid to deal with her kids' problems herself, something poor June refused to do.

In the early 70s, I was intrigued by John Boy's mother on *The Waltons.* Like me, John Boy was a college student studying to be a writer. Though she had six or seven kids, Olivia Walton clearly preferred John Boy to the others. To her, John Boy—despite a mole the size of Rhode Island—could do no wrong and she would always drop whatever she was doing to talk over his problems with him.

"Mama, mama, Jim Bob's cut his arm off at the sawmill."

"Shut up, can't you see I'm talking with my favorite, John Boy?"

From Olivia, I learned that some mothers have favorites. Every kid likes to hope he is the favorite, but, if that's the case, his mother should at least try to hide it, unlike John Boy's.

In the '80s, I spent Friday nights with my rich mom, Miss Ellie, of *Dallas.* A multi-millionaire (oil money), Miss Ellie insisted that her two adult sons and their wives live with her in the same house and share every meal.

Miss Ellie was invariably gracious to her slut of a daughter-in-law, Suellen, who would return home every so often in an alcoholic stupor after a week away in the arms of various lovers. Suellen acted this way to get back at her husband, J.R., who had girlfriends stashed all over town. Not surprisingly, J.R. and Suellen's relationship was volatile.

Surely Miss Ellie wanted to say something but always bit her lip and let J.R. and Suellen work it out. An inspirational example for mothers-in-law everywhere. When my sons bring their future wives home to live with us, I'm going to make sure my wife gives them their privacy, as Miss Ellie did.

My current favorite TV mother is the feisty Livia Soprano of *The Sopranos* on HBO. Last season, Livia tried to arrange to have her middle-aged son, Tony, bumped off by the mob.

From Livia, I've learned that even a mother's supposedly boundless love has its limits, and that every mother, ultimately, has a breaking point.

And so, as we prepare to celebrate Mother's Day, I would like to extend special greetings across the miles not only to my own mother whose failure to breast-feed me has ruined my life, but to each of my boob-tube mothers on whose examples I was weaned.

Thank you, Moms. You've made me the man I am today.

Take good care of yourself (if you can)

Boomers like me are so health conscious these days it's sickening.

All of us want to live long lives, to spend the money we made buying Intel stock (except for those unfortunates whose brokers advised them to *sell* on a *dip* five years ago and, as a result, will have to work in some meaningless job until the day they *die* while the rest of you move to *Florida* at 52 and buy *condos* on golf courses. Not that we're resentful or will take any *perverse pleasure* when we hear you choked to death on an *unpeeled shrimp* from the salad bar at an "Early Bird" special).

Problem is, there's lots of conflicting health-related information going around. You need a Palm Pilot to keep track of the endless stream of factoids you hear on the news. And what's really confusing is that everything we were raised to believe was *bad* for you now seems to now be *good* for you, and vice versa.

Almost every day, new research announced by doctors from places like the University of Northern Saskatchewan or the Center for Disease Control leaves me completely baffled, unable to make intelligent life-or-death decisions about my health.

Last week, for example, I saw a newspaper headline, reporting on research presented at an American Heart Association meeting. It announced, *"Pot smoking linked to sudden heart attacks."* (Not that I've ever touched the stuff, not even the time two fraternity brothers and our dates drove 300 miles in a Camaro to see Cream perform *"Inna Gadda Da Vida"* in concert, and sang along, feeling the meaning of the lyrics with the intensity Lincoln must have felt when he delivered the Gettysburg Address.)

"Smoking marijuana quintuples a person's heart attack risk for an hour after lighting up," the reporter wrote. Made sense so I read on.

"As a heart attack trigger," the next paragraph began, "smoking marijuana is safer than a snort of cocaine or a jolt of intense exercise for a couch potato. "

Say what?

Am I to understand that, given a choice between A) watching *Jeopardy!* while climbing the Stairmaster my wife's been using to dry her pantyhose on for five years because I haven't plugged it in . . . B) snorting cocaine . . . or C) lighting up a joint . . . that "C" is the healthiest choice?

See what I mean?

And that's just the latest conflicting information the American public has been fed.

Who isn't addled about the important role of alcohol in healthcare today?

Everyone knows it's one of the leading causes of alcoholism and can also cause cirrhosis of the liver and other unpleasant side effects. Yet it was revealed last year that a drink or two of hard liquor a day isn't bad for you . . . and it's been reported for years that red wine is actually beneficial, because it helps lower cholesterol. (Warning: After drinking a glass to lower mine, my teeth looked for the next week as though I had just eaten a package of dry Cherry Kool Aid.)

Want more advice?

Newsweek, in its March 6 issue, reported that nicotine may help ease symptoms of depression. (The good news. Everything's coming up roses for you. The bad news. They're for your funeral.)

Then there's all that conflicting nutrition information.

Nobody disputes that carrying around too much weight can strain your heart, not to mention upholstered furniture in other people's homes. The question is, what's the healthiest way to lose unwanted poundage?

To help us sort it out, *Newsweek*, in the same issue, featured a debate that included, among other nutrition experts, Robert Atkins, whose diet plan has sold 10 million books. A typical breakfast on Atkins' regime includes a three-egg omelet and two strips of bacon. For dinner, you can have a steak fried in butter with cream sauce. All this, he claims, actually *lowers* your LDL cholesterol, while making you trim as a marathoner.

What does Atkins do when he's not signing books or debating other diet experts? He's a cardiologist.

I was excited until Dr. Dean Ornish, author of *Eat More, Weigh Less* countered that his "plant-based" diet, resulted in a 40 percent reduction in LDL cholesterol, along with a 91 percent reduction in frequency of chest pain.

So what would you rather be? Greyhound-thin and full as a tick, but with chest pains on Atkins' diet? Or whippet-thin and perpetually hungry, one of those persons who orders oil and vinegar on the side and will live to be 105, making waiters' lives hell, following Ornish's?

I'll take mine medium with extra sour cream and butter on that potato please.

And here's some late-breaking news from last week's Heart Association Conference: Vitamin C pills may cause hardening of the arteries, which can make you forgetful not to menti…

Where was I? Oh yes.

Not all health advice comes from the media. You can pick it up from lots of unexpected sources.

Flying cross-country the other day, I virtuously ordered a can of Bloody Mary mix. I like the taste—it's basically vitamin-packed spicy tomato juice, after all—and thought it a healthier choice than diet cola (made with artificial sweeter which reportedly causes cancer in rats who shouldn't be ingesting all that caffeine anyway). The flight attendant handed it over with a sneer. "You might as well get your day's allotment of salt while you're at it."

Sure enough, the nutrition information on the side of the can proved her right. Percentage of daily recommended sodium: 100.

I said "forget it" and ordered the Absolut Bloody Mary I'd actually wanted to order in the first place, hold the mix.

Healthiest choice I'd made all week.

The boy in the oval picture frame

Atop the bureau in our guest room is a hand-tinted photograph, taken in the summer of 1933.

The photo is of my grandparents, Burton and Judith Tate, and the first four of what would eventually become a brood of 14 grandchildren.

On my grandfather's lap is my cousin Robert, a baby about six months old. Robert grew up to be a computer specialist.

On grandma's lap is my cousin Nancy. She grew up to be an R.N. and had four children of her own.

On the ground in the front of them is my cousin Paul, a boy of six. Paul grew up to marry his childhood sweetheart, and became an Army General. Like his sister Nancy, he had four children.

Next to him is my cousin Jimmy, a boy of four. Jimmy was killed in Korea when he was 21.

I wonder what he would have become?

Nancy, Paul and Jimmy were the children of my mother's sister, Margaret, who never weighed more than 90 pounds in her life. In 1923, tiny Margaret married a giant of a man, Patrick Timmerberg, who stood at least 6 ft. 3 in. Pat's parents had moved to Missouri from Germany, and settled on a farm. When America entered World War I, Pat was shipped off to fight his own people in the fields of France. When he returned, he was a soldier through and through, who loved to sing war songs and tell war stories.

Margaret and Pat's oldest, Paul, joined the army in 1945, the year he graduated from high school, just in time for VJ Day. Like his father, Paul showed a natural aptitude for soldiering. He was selected for Officer Candidate School and, shortly thereafter, was a Lieutenant, on his way to earning his stars.

Jimmy, who graduated from high school in 1947, enlisted in the Army the next year, when he was 19. After basic training, he was sent to Colorado, where he captained the 21st Engineer's Basketball Team. He was shipped to the Yukon for eight months, back to Colorado and in August 1950, to Korea, where he was a machine gunner with the 21st Infantry Regiment of the 24th Division.

Jimmy was killed in action near Changgong-Ni on April 28, 1951. His tour of duty was almost over.

When they received word of Jimmy's death, the Timmerbergs were preparing for Nancy's high school graduation the following week. She had graduated first in her class, and was looking forward to giving the valedictorian's speech.

She went ahead and delivered it, though her heart was broken, and the audience knew it.

In those days before jet planes, families often had to wait months for their loved ones to arrive home for burial. Jimmy's flag-draped casket arrived home in Montgomery City, Missouri, on a Wabash train on November 20, and he was buried with full military honors. According to his obituary posted on cousin Robert's family web site, a quartet sang "In The Sweet By and By" and "Safe In The Arms of Jesus." A solo, "God Understands," was also performed.

My mother was unable to attend. She was in the hospital, having given birth to me three days before.

We visited Aunt Margaret and Uncle Pat often when I was growing up. They were always full of news about Paul and Nancy, and their growing families. Yet I was always aware of a third Timmerberg cousin—a handsome dark-haired boy of 18 or so with a fixed broad smile, who peered from a gold oval frame on the dining room wall. Of him never a word was spoken.

Pat died when I was 11 and Margaret, who lived alone, began spending a lot of time at our house with my mother. They would spend hours discussing the family and events of the past. But they would never mention Jimmy. Every Memorial Day, my mother would take Margaret—who never learned to drive—to the cemetery, and they would return looking grim.

As a teenager, I used to accuse Aunt Margaret of being a pessimist. She always seemed to look on the dark side, to expect the worst out of life.

I take it all back, Aunt Margaret. Now that I'm an adult and have held my own sons in my arms and seen them become teenagers with hopes and dreams of their own, I understand. And I want to tell you this: You were amazing. I don't know how you were able to go on, but you did. You even laughed on occasion. I can't help but wonder if, every time you saw me, you were reminded of the hell you were living the week I was being born.

Margaret died in 1986, and was laid to rest next to Jimmy and Pat, near my grandparents' graves. My mother, now 87, still makes the 50-mile pilgrimage to the cemetery every Memorial Day. And while she is close to Paul and Nancy and talks about them often, she never, ever, speaks of Jimmy. Nobody in the family does. I don't think those who knew him can.

Many of my grandparents' 14 grandchildren accomplished great things. One became a math professor. One went to West Point and earned a law degree. One, named for his cousin Jimmy, is president of a major music company. All of us married, most had children, and four are now grandparents themselves.

Scattered from Connecticut to California, all of us will celebrate Memorial Day. We'll enjoy the sunshine and barbeques.

And I guarantee that, on Monday, each of us will remember the boy in the oval picture frame in Aunt Margaret's dining room, the boy who, unlike the rest of us, never grew old.

I hope that, whatever else you have planned, you will also take a moment to remember Jimmy, the hundreds of thousands of other boys who never made it home, and their parents, who buried the best of themselves with them.

Lost in spaciness

I'm a loser.

You name it, I've lost it.

I lost my high school class ring an hour after I received it. Seven years later I lost my wedding ring. On my honeymoon.

I've lost things all over the world. Airline tickets in South Africa. Travelers' cheques in Brazil. Prescription sunglasses in Mississippi, China and Morocco.

I've lost more cell phones than I can count, most recently last month when I left my latest Star-Tac either in a rental car, my hotel room or a restaurant booth in Pensacola. Or maybe I left it in the Delta Crowne Room when changing planes at the Atlanta airport on the way home. I'm not sure. I think it was in my briefcase. That's missing, too.

I bought a Palm Pilot Organizer to help me keep track of things, but it disappeared.

At the office, I lose papers constantly. Co-workers know never to give me an original document. They make four or five copies of any paper I need to see, knowing I'll come asking for a duplicate, then a duplicate of that. Our employee handbook instructs new hires not to give Tom anything original.

1-800-492-3344 is a number I know by heart. It's the number you call to report lost American Express cards, and I'm on a first-name basis with the people on the other end. (Wanda, by the way, recently gave birth to a healthy 8-pound girl, which was a relief. The last two times I called, she told me the baby was in a breech position. I heard this happy news yesterday when I called to ask AmEx to cancel my latest lost card. I found it five minutes after I hung up. It was under my car seat, along with a cell phone I had lost earlier this year.)

I lose my wallet and car keys every day but that's not my fault. I always place them on the breakfast room table when I come home, but somebody breaks in during the night and hides them some place where I can't find them the next morning. This has happened every night for 30 years and it's starting to annoy me.

What makes me this way? Because I come from a long line of losers, all of whom share a defective gene inherited from my maternal grandmother, the Queen of all Losers.

In the 1950s, her children chipped in to send grandma aboard the Queen Mary to Europe, which she had dreamed of visiting for 70 years. Somewhere between New York and Southhampton, she lost her passport. British Customs officials wouldn't allow her to disembark so she had to turn around and sail back to America. All she ever saw of Europe was the view from the ship's deck.

Anyway, The Gene my mother, her siblings, their children, grandchildren and great-grandchildren inherited renders us all incapable of keeping track of anything in our possession.

We actually believe The Gene goes farther back than grandma, and would like to trace it back through our lineage, but someone lost the family Bible in which births, deaths and marriages were faithfully recorded from 1701 onward. My mother accuses Aunt Betty. Betty says Cousin Joe had it last. Personally, I think it's in the safe in my mother's front hall closet, to which she lost the combination years ago.

When our extended family of losers gathers from far and wide, as we did for my niece's wedding, it can be too much, even for me. All of us were staying in a hotel. An hour before the wedding, Aunt Dorothy realized she had left her room key in her purse, which was in cousin Reba's room. Reba's room key, in turn, was in her jacket pocket, which was in cousin Paul's car. Paul had left the keys to his car, which contained two of the bridesmaid dresses in the trunk, in Dorothy's room.

The wedding was supposed to start at 3, but didn't start until 4:30. Our family motorcade got lost en route to the church, because cousin Steve, who was driving the lead car, had misplaced the printed map.

We always take such delays in stride. If we are going somewhere, we automatically factor into our timetable an extra 10 to 20 minutes to look for keys, glasses and wallets. We even laugh about it and say our spaciness about possessions proves we're preoccupied with loftier thoughts.

But there's one member of the family who isn't amused. My wife. She has never misplaced a thing in her life and doesn't understand how or why we do.

Her punishment for being terminally organized has been to give birth to two sons who inherited The Gene.

Our 17-year-old wears a New York Knicks hat 18 hours a day, but it disappears every night, so our family spends 10 minutes looking for it every morning. Our younger son has lost his shoes every morning for 14 years, and they never turn up in the same place. I have a theory that the same poltergeist who's hiding my keys and wallet is also hiding my sons' caps and shoes.

Knowing how organized my wife is, I do feel sorry for her, but she knew I came from a long line of losers before we were married. When our antics make her so frustrated she threatens to walk, I like to remind her of a line from *The Godfather*. "You can never lose your family."

But actually, that's not true. My brother once left his 3-year-son in a store and didn't notice the child was missing until he arrived home. My sister-in-law was horrified when her husband walked in the door without the boy.

They lived in Germany at the time, and the store was two hours away. In Luxembourg.

Your call is important to us. You aren't.

I have a client in a city about 500 miles away I visit often. I usually fly there in the morning . . . meet . . . and return home in the late afternoon.

My client, however, sometimes prefers to meet bright and early. And so, when I need to be there before 9 a.m., I fly down the night before

Last week, I was scheduled to make a presentation early Tuesday.

So, I made reservations for the 6 p.m. flight Monday. I planned to get to my hotel around 8, order room service, watch a Spectravision movie, then enjoy a full eight hours of sleep.

It was not to be. At 5:30 p.m. Monday, my staff and I were still running around like chickens without heads, pulling together the presentation, and it looked like we still had at least two hours of work ahead of us. Knowing I was going to miss my flight, I called the airline to find out when the last plane of the evening departed.

Here's the recorded message I heard.

"Thank you for calling U-Fly Airways, where we put U first. All our agents are busy now, but your call is important to us. To

help expedite your call, choose from one of the following menu options.

If you are calling from a pay toilet, press 1.

If you are calling from a rotary phone, you're probably elderly and shouldn't be flying anyway since your artificial hip will set off metal detectors, so hang up now and call Amtrak.

If you are calling from a touchtone phone, press 2." I pressed 2.

"*If you are a member of our frequent flyer program, press 1.*"

I did.

"*Please enter your 12-digit account number.*"

I didn't know it off the top of my head. There was 10 seconds of silence. I started thinking I would have to call back and choose another option. To my relief, the voice continued.

"*If you don't know your number, please choose from the following.*

For awards travel in the U.S., press 1.

For awards travel to Europe, press 2.

For awards travel on our new nonstops from Cleveland to Saskatoon or Monrovia, press 3.

If you think you will get an awards ticket to fly within 1,000 miles of your destination within a month of the time you plan to travel, press the pound key and ask for Santa Claus.

If you are not traveling on an awards ticket, press 4."

I pressed 4. The cheery voice continued.

"*To make reservations for travel within the next seven days, press 1.*

For gate information on today's arriving flights, press 2.

To change reservations for travel within the U.S., please press 3."

I pressed 3.

The airline's theme song began playing. And another recorded message began.

"*Due to our mega-saver fares, we are experiencing unprecedented call volume. Please stay on the line . . . and choose from one of the following options.*

For lost or misplaced luggage, press 1.

If you are calling from a pay phone in the Minneapolis airport where flights are canceled due to inclement weather, and think that, by calling this number, you can avoid the line at the counter that extends all the way to the Mall of America, proceed directly to the Cheers bars on Concourse A and order a double Tanqueray martini for us, we need one.

If you were aboard flight 77 November 29th and are calling about the brunette flight attendant with PMS, please press 2 for a free headset coupon redeemable on your next flight.

If you are a food service vendor who has figured out how to prevent the bags of Fritos we serve with a half-bologna sandwich in our first class cabin from exploding at 35,000 feet, press 3.

If you are calling about the brick-size package found in the lavatory ceiling on flight 99 from Medellin to Miami yesterday, press 4 and ask for Jose.

If you are the funeral director who has been calling hourly for the last two days, good news. We've located your missing cargo in Omaha. You can tell the family Uncle Frank will be arriving at JFK tomorrow on flight 35 at 12.32 p.m.

If you are calling on a cell phone from an aircraft that has landed in Minneapolis and is parked at the gate, and wish to find out when you will be deplaning, please be advised that none of our jetway operators could get to work today. Even in Minneapolis where it snows half the year, they don't drive four-wheel-drive SUVs that guzzle more gas than our 747s like those crazy people in Wilton, Connecticut. So put your seat back, and have a pleasant evening.

For departure information on today's flights, please press 6."

I pressed 6.

"Please enter your flight number."

I didn't know my flight number or when it would leave—that's why I was calling in the first place.

"If you don't know your flight number, please stay on the line. Or, for faster service, visit our website at ufly.com.

The theme song began again.

Just then, I was handed a packed portfolio of work to present at my meeting. I slammed down the phone, hopped in my car, and raced to LaGuardia at 80 miles per hour.

When I arrived, I found the last flight of the evening had been cancelled. The counter agent didn't know how why, and had no suggestions.

So I called another airline, to see if I could catch one of its flights.

"Thank you for calling," the recorded voice said. *"Due to inclement weather in the Minneapolis area, our reservationists are busy assisting other travelers. But please stay on the line, your call is important to us."*

Gimme a head with hair

It's Saturday night as I write this. We had planned to go out to dinner, but my wife refuses to be seen in public with me. She says she won't be seen anywhere with someone who looks like he just escaped from prison. So here I sit, writing a column instead.

It started in May, when I was stalked by a stranger during a trip to London.

As I always do in big cities, I walked everywhere, stopping often to look in store windows.

Every time I stopped, I saw the stalker's reflection. With his white hair and mustache, his resemblance to my grandfather—a man I know only from photographs—was uncanny. And he was dressed exactly like me, who, when I looked closer, wasn't in the reflected image at all. Only him.

It struck me I've lost the right to write "brown" under "hair color" on driver's license and passport applications. It must have happened so gradually I didn't notice it.

Observing the stalker carefully, I noted he was actually rather distinguished-looking. But who the hell wants to look distinguished in their 40s? At 70, sure. But I'm not ready to wear that moniker. Not yet.

Don't get me wrong, I'm not complaining. At least I have hair. Lots of men my age lost most of theirs years ago. While friends debate the merits of Rogaine versus Propecia, I order another beer. Mine isn't even receding. It's just white.

Anyway, about the time I was noticing the old geezer stalking me through London, I began observing that almost all the businessmen in Jolly Old—young and old alike—are wearing their hair short these days. Not Marine Corps-short, but short—maybe an inch or so, all around.

It occurred to me that, if I were to have mine cut short, white hair would no longer be the first thing people notice about me. I'd once again look like the 25-year-old I actually am, who just happens to be trapped inside a 48-year-old body.

Walking through Soho my final afternoon, it started to rain. I looked up, saw a "barber" sign and ducked inside. Luck was with me; a regular had just called to cancel an appointment. I plopped down in the barber's chair, pointed to a customer in the next chair with a 1" all-around haircut and said, "Give me a cut like that."

I flew home the next day. My wife liked my new look.

That night, to further enhance my new youthful appearance, I impulsively shaved off the mustache I've worn since I was 18.

Years disappeared down the drain along with the whiskers.

A few weeks later, I decided to get a trim. So I went to the stylist who's cut my hair for years. She did a great job, using barber clippers instead of the scissors the London barber had used. She said there was nothing to it; all she had to do was set the dial to an inch length, and run the clippers over my head. I returned several times over the summer.

Which brings me to a few hours ago. I won't tell you where this incident of depraved de-butchery took place. But beware. It could happen to you.

All week I had been intending to get a haircut because I have an important new business meeting Monday and want to look my spiffiest. When I finally called around noon today, my regular stylist was booked solid.

While running errands, I saw an "open" sign at a barber

shop I had visited 10 or so years ago and which, after the barber had completely disregarded my instructions, I swore I would never visit again. But then I thought, "All I have to do is ask him to adjust the clippers to an inch setting. There's nothing to it." So I walked into the shop.

I instructed, "The woman I usually go to sets the clippers to an inch and cuts it the same length all around."

He turned on the clippers, and before I could stop him, merrily buzzed a deep swath along either side of my scalp.

"What are you doing?"

"Bitches don't know how to cut men's hair."

"I look like Mr. T."

"You wait, this is gonna be the best haircut you ever had."

He proceeded to give me a buzz cut like the one I was given my first day at Wentworth Military Academy when I was 16. He had to finish once he started, to make the rest of it as short as the swath he had cut along the sides of my head. It took all of two minutes.

He did not receive a tip.

I stopped at a store on the way home and ran into a friend. "That's some haircut," she said, suppressing a grin. "Makes you look younger."

I called my wife on the car phone to give her a—pardon the pun—heads-up.

When I arrived home, the kids roared with laughter. My wife, aghast, said we weren't going anywhere together tonight or in the foreseeable future.

So here I sit, writing a column. My hair is approximately as long as my whiskers would be if I didn't shave for a day. There are birthmarks on my scalp I never knew I had.

We had planned to go to our favorite restaurant here in town tonight. I was looking forward to it.

But then, I don't want my readers to see me and think I've become a neo-Nazi skinhead. Or have landed the Daddy Warbucks role in the next remake of *Annie.*

I'm still me.

And I hope to be able to show my face in public by Thanksgiving.

Barking up the wrong tree

My wife and I are bursting with pride. Our girl has been invited to join the board of the Planned Parenthood Action Fund, the political arm of the Planned Parenthood Federation.

I can't begin to tell you how much this honor means to us. We've never told anyone, but in her reckless youth, our girl gave birth to four out-of-wedlock offspring. Her invitation is proof-positive she has turned her life around and that her fellow Action Fund members—including Whoppi Goldberg, Sarah-Jessica Parker and Barbra Streisand—recognize she has learned enough from her painful experience to help other young mothers-to-be make informed choices.

Unfortunately, she won't be able to attend any meetings. Besides, she's no longer concerned about family planning. The Humane Society insisted she be spayed before we could bring her home with us.

How did Bella, the sad-eyed beagle we found in the pound, where she had given birth to four puppies, receive such a prestigious invitation?

Because we subscribe—make that subscribed, it recently folded—to *George*, the political magazine founded by JFK, Jr. But not in our names. In Bella's full name—Bella Dina Dryden.

Most magazines supplement their incomes by selling subscriber lists to marketers. *George* obviously sold its list to Planned Parenthood, which figured that most *George* subscribers would support its goals. Planned Parenthood, in turn, sent out a mailing to female subscribers in selected high-income zip codes, including Bella Dina in 06897, inviting them to sit on the board . . . and, by the way, to cough up some serious bucks for the honor.

All Bella can cough up is yellow foam and, on occasion, squirrel body parts.

How, you ask, can I be sure the list came from *George*? Because *George* is the only magazine Bella ever subscribed to as Bella Dina Dryden.

She gets *Readers' Digest* as plain old Bella Dryden, and *People* as B.D. Dryden.

In all, we take 15 magazines in the names or nicknames of Bella . . . Clyde, our idiot dachshund . . . and Ocean, a buck-toothed 15-pound mongrel we found starving on a beach in Aruba and brought to America. He, alas, passed on to that big boneyard in the sky summer before last, but we can't bring ourselves to change his subscriptions.

As regular readers of this column know, my bread and butter is direct marketing—junk mail to you. My agency's job is to create irresistible offers for our clients; to write, design and produce the mailings; and to search for the ideal combination of mailing lists, many of which are compiled from the names of magazine subscribers.

For years, because I like to see which magazines are selling their lists and to whom, I've subscribed to magazines in the names of the dogs, so I can yuk it up when mail starts arriving for them.

Ocean (a.k.a. Otie Van der Root Dryden) the other day received a personal invitation from "The Office of the Governor of Alaska" informing him he was eligible to receive an official Alaska Travel Guide, "as bold and exciting as Alaska."

"Just imagine," Governor Tony Knowles wrote, "a dog sled

ride or Eskimo blanket toss, panning for gold, relaxing in fine restaurants."

Ocean hated the cold and was deathly afraid of large dogs, so the dog sled ride wouldn't have appealed to him. He would, however, have loved "relaxing in fine restaurants." He spent much of his pre-Wilton life on the sidewalk in front of the open-air restaurant at the Hyatt in Aruba, begging patrons to throw food to him. He would have appreciated being invited inside a restaurant where, perhaps, he could have gotten a VIP table by dropping the name of his pal, Tony Knowles.

And he could have used his MBNA Platinum MasterCard to fly to his gala Alaskan holiday, because yesterday he received a letter announcing he was "pre-approved for a spending limit of up to $10,000." Last time he flew, he was crated, inside the cargo hold of an Air Aruba jet. This time, using his Platinum MasterCard, he could have brought along his best buddy, Clyde, and they could have flown first-class.

Of all our dogs, Ocean, who spent his formative years abroad, fittingly receives the most travel-related mail. That's because we subscribe to *Conde Nast Traveler* and *National Geographic Traveler* using two of his nicknames. In recent months he has received double cabin category upgrades from Cunard on selected QE II transatlantic cruises, and, most impressive of all, was invited by Mercedes-Benz to pick up his next custom-built Mercedes at the factory in Stuttgart, and to take it for a spin around Europe.

And to think he was a flea-covered vagrant living under a bush when we found him.

Clyde gets the most sports mail, thanks to his subscriptions to *ESPN Magazine* and *Sports Illustrated.*

Bella, on the other hand, is our political animal. She was invited recently by Senator Edward Kennedy to attend a special Democratic National Committee planning session to strategize the party's future provided, of course, she contributed $1,000.

I'm sure she would have contributed a lot of outside-the-box thinking—perhaps a tax holiday for families who adopt dogs from animal shelters—that could have put the Democrats back in the White House in 2004.

She wanted to go, I could tell, because she took the invitation from the trash can, where I had tossed it, and placed it at my feet expectantly, like Lassie fetching Timmy's slippers. But I had just cut off her allowance as punishment for all the holes she had joyfully dug in our front yard, and Clyde wouldn't lend her his American Express Optima card because it's framed and hanging on the bathroom wall where he can't get to it.

"Life's a bitch," I told Bella, as she sulked on the sofa.

"And, come to think of it, so are you."

Take me out to the ball game

Take me out to the ball game, take me out with the crowd. Buy me some peanuts and Crackerjack. Then hit me over the head with a brick and wake me when it's over. Please.

This may sound un-American—even unmanly. But I hate baseball. Next to the annual colonoscopy I have to endure because of a family history of unpleasantness in that netherworld, Major League baseball is my least favorite pastime.

Come to think of it, the anesthesiologist at least knocks me out for the colonoscopy; I don't remember a thing when I wake up.

The game I remember in excruciating detail, from the stop-and-go traffic that begins 10 miles from the stadium . . . to the "da-da-da-da, dada!" the organist trills endlessly to keep the crowd awake . . . to the tattooed woman wearing a Derek Jeter jersey in the row behind me two years ago who downed four hot dogs with kraut, two bags of peanuts and seven Budweisers, then projectile-vomited during the seventh inning stretch.

Then there's the three or four-hour game itself, which I can never see because I'm sitting at least half a mile away, not that I want to. It always goes into extra innings whenever I'm in attendance.

My aversion to baseball goes back to my childhood when I

played Little League in a baseball-obsessed small town. Because my father's store sponsored the team and provided the uniforms, the coach had to let me play at least one inning every game.

A little butterball with bad eyesight, I was relegated to right field, where I would pass the time on my knees looking for four-leaf clovers, until I'd hear a "thwack" and the crowd would start yelling, "Look up, look up!" I always extended my glove straight out in front of me . . . put the other hand over my face to protect it . . . ran zombie-like toward the ball I could never see coming but the crowd's roar assured me was on its way . . . and missed it by a mile every time.

Needless to say, I usually incurred the wrath not only of my teammates, but of their parents who, by the ninth inning when I was finally allowed to play, had consumed a couple of six-packs of Schlitz.

I wasn't any good at it, so I decided at an early age that baseball and I were not simpatico. If other guys wanted to spend their summers watching grown men wearing flannel uniforms and knee socks, that was their business. I figured I attended my last game in 1963, when I was bused with my fellow School Boy Patrolmen to a Kansas City Athletics game. I think they played the Brooklyn Dodgers. Maybe it was the Mets.

As payback, the Lord—who Himself must be a fan or at least has a wicked sense of humor—sent unto me two sons who live and breathe baseball. From the time the leaves start budding in April, until they fall in October, my boys commandeer the family room to watch every game on the tube. I always go to the opposite end of the house, and shut the doors in a vain attempt to drown out the shouts and screams.

Naturally, my sons don't root for the same team. One is a Yankees fan, the other loves the Mets. But of course, no matter which of their teams is playing, they watch every game together, so they can argue loudly about whose team is best.

As if I weren't punished enough, my only brother—the guy with whom I supposedly share more genes than anyone—is a baseball fanatic. He spends every March in Florida at the Cincinnati Reds training camp, never misses a Reds home game and spouts statistics constantly. When Pete Rose was sent up the river, he grieved as if it were his own son. His e-mail address is UltimateRedsFan.

No matter how hard I try to steer the conversation away from it, he always brings it back to baseball. I'll say, for instance, "Doesn't Uncle Herb look natural? It's almost as if he's asleep." He'll reply, "I remember a Cardinals game Uncle Herb took me to in 1956. That was the year Stan Musial had an ERA of 401, an RBI average of 853, and a 401(k) of 92.3."

Every year, the boys prevail upon me to take them to a game. They start in early April, by checking schedules on the Internet and leaving printouts around the house listing games—usually double-headers—for which tickets are available. I try to ignore them.

Then I start feeling guilty, remembering other fathers who work for big corporations that have box seats and whose kids get to go to the ballpark so often they're on a first name basis with players.

And so, invariably on the hottest day of the year, I find myself in the car with the boys, headed to Shea or Yankee Stadium. I take my Walkman along, and listen to a book on tape. Other fans who see me with headphones think I'm tuned into the game when, in fact, I'm listening to the latest John Grisham or Stephen King novel.

Last summer my brother flew to New York to visit his only son, who had just taken a job in Manhattan. He called, said he knew how much my boys loved baseball, and suggested we meet at Shea. I hadn't seen my brother in a year, it was time for the kids' annual pilgrimage, so off we went.

When we settled in our seats, my brother and sons immediately began trying to one-up each other by reciting statistics about players on the field. I put on my headphones. My 29-year-old nephew—the son of the ultimate baseball fan—looked over at me, grinned, and pulled out a paperback, which he read the entire game.

The Lord sho 'nuff has a sense of humor, doesn't He?

Living off the fat of the land

I was shocked to open the paper the other morning and see headlines proclaiming a national "epidemic of obesity."

I almost gagged on my Entenmann's Chocolate-Covered Doughnut.

Not because I was surprised at the news, but by the stupidity of it all since my tax dollars were used to fund a definitive study which proved Americans are getting heavier.

This news flash also gave me pause because I'm still eating Butterfingers from Halloween and plan to sit down tomorrow and stuff my piehole with turkey, dressing and pecan pie until I stagger into the family room and pass out in front of the TV.

When I wake up, I'll make myself a turkey sandwich I'll top with cheese and garnish with Miracle Whip Light. (I have to draw the line somewhere).

For my grand Thanksgiving finale, I'll eat the last piece of pie without even going through the pretense of putting it on a plate.

And so, intrigued, I reached for another doughnut and continued reading.

According to the study, a record number—17.9%—of all adults now qualify as "obese." This information was obtained by calling a random group of 100,000 Americans, who were asked their height and weight. Researchers noted the actual incidence of obesity is likely higher because people tend to exaggerate their height and shave off a few pounds. (I remember overhearing my wife on the phone telling someone she was 6 ft. 2 in. and 106 lbs. Now I understand.)

The article thoughtfully provided a formula so readers would be able to determine if they, too, are obese. It went something like this. Multiply your height by .056473, then divide your weight in Kilograms by the current temperature at JFK. The result will tell you if you're obese or not.

My question is this: Who did these researchers call? They sure didn't call the small town where I grew up in Missouri. If they had, they'd know there's no way 17.9% of the population of that town is obese. It's more like 100%.

When I went to my 25th high school reunion a few years ago, I was the thinnest person there—male or female. And at 182 lbs. and 6 ft. tall, I'm not exactly the male counterpart of Calista Flockhart.

Folks there aren't merely well-fed, they're massive. And growing more so by the minute.

I watched one classmate—a formerly petite little bookworm who now possesses bosoms the size of my head—polish off a plate of spareribs and potato salad in three minutes flat, which she washed down with two non-diet Cokes. When she was finished, the bones on the plate looked like a carcass picked clean by buzzards.

Out there, nobody notices if you're sucking fat from bones like an Electrolux, because they're all busy doing the same thing.

And to think I was worried about a little extra sag in my jawline.

In most of the Midwest, the concept of a fat-free or low-fat diet is just that: A concept. Something of concern to high-strung easterners and youth-obsessed Californians, like capital gains taxes and SUV leather interior options.

In a one-mile stretch of highway in St. Charles, Missouri, I recently noted a McDonald's, Pizza Hut, White Castle, Burger King, Dunkin' Donuts, Lion's Choice Roast Beef, Steak & Shake, A&W, Arby's, Hardees, KFC, Baskin-Robbins, Sonic Drive-In and Taco Bell, all abuzz with activity at 9 p.m. Happy families, having their after-supper snacks.

Having lived east of the Hudson half my life, and in the Midwest the rest, I'm astonished at the differences between the way people eat here and there. Especially people in a well-off town like Wilton, who can afford to eat whatever they want but don't because they're afraid they'll put on a pound or two. And so, when they go out to dinner, they order baked scrod.

When I get off a plane in Missouri, I know I'm home immediately by the people happily waddling through the airport. It's like I've landed in a Botero painting. Everyone, by and large, is huge. The women look like suomo wrestlers in stretch pants. The men carry pot bellies that hover over their belts, as if they might crash to the floor any minute.

It's a stark contrast to LaGuardia, where whippet-thin businesswomen and trim, well-tailored men whip out their cell phones and start cutting deals as they rush to their waiting Lincoln Town Cars.

I was on safari in Africa earlier this year. At my camp table one evening were four other baby-boomers—a cardiologist, originally from South Africa who now lives in Ohio, a woman from France, and a couple from London. The doctor was describing to everyone's amusement how, in America, boomers are obsessed with eating right, staying fit, and how everyone knows their cholesterol levels.

The French woman wasn't familiar with the term. The English couple admitted they had been meaning to get theirs checked but hadn't gotten around to it. The doctor turned to me and said, "I bet Tom here knows both his good and his bad cholesterol numbers." I did.

"Funny thing about affluent Americans, "he said. "They're all starving themselves, eating no-fat foods so they'll live to be

110. What they don't realize is that they'll spend the last 30 of those years in a nursing home, wishing they hadn't."

That hit home. As did a friend's recent premature death which reminded me—big time—that life is too short and is meant to be savored now, not at some future date we may not live to see.

So when you sit down at your table tomorrow, thank the good Lord you're here to enjoy it and, for once in your life, *eat.*

Eat a lot.

Eat everything on the table, then have a piece of pie with Haagen-Dazs or whipped cream on top. And when you're finished, have another.

You can always work it off Friday, if you're lucky enough to wake up. If not, you'll die contented.

And if, by chance, you have any leftover pie, call me. I'll be right over.

Who says it's more blessed to give?

For most folks, the holiday season is a time of joy and giving.

For me, it's a time of abject terror.

That's because I hate to shop, and I don't need a shrink to tell me why.

It all goes back to my childhood.

My father owned a general store that sold thousands of items but, to conserve space, only one brand and style of each item.

If you wanted a pair of jeans, there was one choice: Lee.

If you needed a pair of shoes, it was Endicott-Johnson or nothing.

My family wasn't allowed to buy anything anywhere else, unless Dryden's Store didn't sell it. And, since we sold most everything, shopping for us was easy.

Because I had no choices as a child, today, when I walk into a department store or—worse yet—a mall, I go into sensory overload.

If a store offered, say, one red sweater, no problem, I'd buy it. But when I'm confronted with dozens of choices—cashmere, wool, cotton, cardigan, crew-neck, v-neck, cowl-neck, et al—I'm so boggled I can't decide.

And so, nine times out of ten, I leave empty-handed.

Mercifully, my wife, who's an expert shopper, always takes care of buying the kids' Christmas presents and signs my name on the "to/from" cards. I look as forward to Christmas morning as they do, so I can see what video games we'll be playing over the coming year.

And buying for my mother is a snap. She loves biographies. One stop in the non-fiction section of the bookstore (or, better yet, at amazon.com), and she's taken care of.

So the only person I really have to shop for is my wife.

"Now Tom," you say, "that shouldn't be too hard."

Au contraire. Sure, Christmas is nine whole days away. But her birthday is today. Worse yet, our anniversary is December 27th. So I have to cram an entire year's worth of shopping and giving into eleven days, during the busiest time of year.

This year I thought I'd gotten off easy.

For the first time ever, my wife told me exactly what she wants—a one-of-a-kind bracelet we admired this summer in a St. Martin jewelry store. After we left the store, I made up an excuse about leaving my sunglasses on the counter, went back, and had the sales clerk write down the exact description of the item. I told the clerk I'd call in November to order it.

Alas, last month St. Martin was struck by Hurricane Lenny. I read in the paper that the beachfront street on which the jeweler was located was inundated by a storm surge. I've tried to rouse the store by both phone and e-mail ever since. I'm afraid that beautiful bracelet may be sleeping with the fishes at the bottom of the Caribbean Sea.

And so, this past Saturday, I found myself at the mall.

Within minutes after arriving, I noticed a store selling Brunswick pool tables.

OK, I know my wife doesn't want a pool table, but I do.

I spent a half hour discussing the various makes, models, wood trim and felt cover color options with the salesman, convincing myself I could talk my wife into letting me turn the dining room, which we never use anyway, into a pool room.

Realizing I had to be home in four hours, I told the salesman I'd be back . . . and plunged into Macy's, where Lady Luck was with me.

Over the next two hours I purchased a beautiful cableknit turtleneck . . . a microfiber blue blazer that's a perfect match for my wife's eyes . . . and an elegantly-tailored winter coat.

If I may say so myself, I look terrific in all of them. (Hey, we have parties to go to, I need to look my best.)

But I saw nothing I thought she would like.

Leaving Macy's feeling guilty, I wandered, as I do every year, into The Sharper Image, where I spent a half hour trying out the $3,999 vibrating massage chairs to relieve my holiday stress. I even filled out an entry for the chance to win one. I hope I do, but I bet I won't.

I went into a record store to see if my wife's favorite group had released a new CD. Just as I walked in, the kid behind the counter, wearing three studs through his eyebrows, cranked up Celine Dion screeching "O Holy Night" which sounded to me like fingernails being drawn across a chalkboard. I hightailed it out of there.

Running low on time, I ducked into another department store where painted, sweet-smelling women were attempting to lure passing men to their cosmetic counters. "Come over here and I'll throw in a gift-wrapped sampler of our holiday lipsticks and matching nail enamels for just $19.99 with any fragrance purchase," one said, winking at me. I felt like a sailor in the red-light district of Amsterdam. And since my mama always told me to stay away from women who looked like that, I turned and fled.

So I arrived home with a bagful of stuff for me, nothing for her. And with the knowledge that I will probably wind up, as I do every year, closing down the mall on December 24th.

At sundown Christmas Eve, while the rest of you are attending worship services and making precious memories with your family, I'll still be at the damned mall, begging store managers not to turn out their lights and pull down their steel gates, and making irrational purchases like the "Funeral of Princess Diana" videotape I gave my wife two years ago.

I told her I thought it was romantic and historical, and that it was something she would want to watch over and over.

She thanked me sweetly, and took it back the day after Christmas, along with just about everything else I had bought at the last minute.

As she no doubt will again this year.

37-DRYD

The man's guide to a festive holiday season

Martha Stewart has become a gazillionaire writing columns and books, publishing a magazine and hosting TV and radio shows in which she advises women how to make the holiday season more festive.

We men celebrate the holidays too, and we don't care about the things Martha and her minions worry so much about, like making centerpieces. We have our own holiday concerns, but nobody has come forward with advice for us, have they?

Well, they have now. Here is chapter one of *Doubting Thomas' Holiday Guide For Men.* Look for my coffee-table book next year. And a TV show the year after that. Then I'm going public. I'll let you in on the IPO.

"My wife always drags me to church on Christmas Eve. I feel like a hypocrite, especially when the minister makes some snide remark about my presence being as rare as snow in June. How can I get out of this annual ritual?"

At noon on Christmas Eve, start complaining about a sore throat. Mention it every hour on the hour until around 4 p.m., at which point say you have the chills and need to lie down. When the wife and kids leave for church, that's the time to run to the mall or Wal-Mart and start your holiday shopping.

"When invited to holiday open houses, what should I bring along as a thanks for the hospitality?"

For some reason, people always seem to take gifts for the hostess. Why not for the host? After all, we men are the ones who've been vacuuming, moving furniture, buying the liquor and schlepping the plates and glasses from Taylor Rental while our better half has been in the bedroom trying on dozens of black dresses that look just alike anyway. I always keep on hand for this purpose a gift-wrapped supply of Turbo-Groomer Battery-Powered Nose and Ear Hair Trimmers I buy on sale at The Sharper Image.

"I can never get our Christmas tree to stand up straight. I've tried placing books under the legs of the stand to level the tree but once we put the star on top, the tree tumbles over, breaking half the ornaments and causing the kids to burst into tears. What can I do?"

Simple. Construct a square box out of 2 x 6 pieces of lumber. Buy a bag of Redi-Mixi Concrete and follow the instructions. Just as it is about to set, stick the tree in it and it will stand up as straight as a redwood.

"I'm a manly man, and feel extremely uncomfortable singing the 'Don we now our gay apparel' line from 'Deck The Halls' when gathered around the piano at holiday parties. Can you tell me the origins of this curious phrase?"

"Deck The Halls" is an olde English song. The line in question was added in 1649 by the Liverpool Gaye Men's Chorus.

"Can you suggest an appropriate gift for a valued client?"

I've found that a personal note, in which you tell the client how much his business has meant, and that you've opened a Swiss bank account into which you've deposited funds equivalent to 5% of the revenue he generated for your company, is always appreciated. Be sure to provide the account number.

"I hate to shop and get addled when confronted with dozens of choices. What should I buy my wife?"

Here's an idea. On Christmas morning after the kids have unwrapped Santa's presents and you've unwrapped yet another sweater you'll never wear, take her aside and point out that the two of you live in an affluent town, have a lovely stretch-colonial, and 2.3 perfect children. Explain that you, like most men, have trouble shopping, that she already has three closets full of clothes, four pashmina shawls and a late-model SUV. Tell her she is God's gift to you 365 days a year, that you adore her and that your wish for her is happiness, health and joy in the coming year. If she buys that, you've saved yourself a mint. If she doesn't, pull out of your bathrobe pocket a picture of a piece of jewelry you've printed out from Internet, and tell her it was on back-order. Worked for me! Once.

"Like Ben Stiller's character in Meet the Parents, I'm Jewish, my fiancee is Christian. My ultra-devout future father-in-law wants to know which December holiday his grandkids will celebrate. What should I tell him?"

Kwanzaa.

"Our dog always hikes his leg on the Christmas tree. What do you suggest?"

Put yourself in his paws. You're a *dog*. Your master brings a tree, like the ones you were praised for relieving yourself on when you were being house-broken, into your living environment, then yells when you do what you were trained to do. No wonder Fido is confused.

Here's how I solve the problem. Place all gifts on a table out of the line of fire, and drape a plastic dry cleaning bag around the base of the tree. And for Pete's sake, don't place the tree on a good rug.

"My hand-wrapped gifts always look terrible. I just don't have a flair for gift-wrapping like women do. Suggestions?"

Give money. That's what everyone is going to exchange your gifts for anyway. Stash the cash in a Hallmark card and write the recipient's name on the envelope. Nobody will complain about your sloppy handwriting, believe me.

"I identify strongly with the Jimmy Stewart character in 'It's a Wonderful Life.' Like him at Christmastime, I experience major business stress, my kids drive me crazy, and sometimes I wish I hadn't been born. Am I unusual?"

No, you're a man. Get down on your knees and thank the good Lord you don't worry about centerpieces.

samX yrreM

For most people I know, Christmas is a time to celebrate life, the birth of a Savior. It's time to spend with family and friends, to bask in good cheer, to count blessings. Christmas brings out the best in most people.

I am not one of them.

To me, Christmas isn't about life. It's about death, and every year is a struggle to get through it.

No violins please, but my father died when I was 14. During Christmas of 1965, he was a living skeleton, as ill as a human can be and still be classified as alive. He died shortly thereafter, but to me he actually died that Christmas night when the ambulance took him away and he never came home again.

My father ran a small town general store. Like many men of his generation, his work was his life . . . and he worked six days a week, 14 hours a day. If I wanted to spend time with him, I had to go where he was. So, like my older brother and sister before me, I started clerking at the store when I was eight. Every afternoon after school, I would report to the store and stay until 7 p.m., closing time.

Christmas was a magical time to work in a country store. Not only did we sell exotic seasonal specialties like Brazil nuts, tangerines, egg nog and satiny ribbon-shaped candies, we were stocked to the rafters with toys and practical Midwestern types of gifts—scratchy flannel shirts, stocking caps, rubber galoshes, long underwear and the like.

Dryden's Store had a large showroom window, facing the town's main street. My father let me decorate it each year, and it was the highlight of my holiday.

First, I would build a fireplace out of cardboard bricks. From the mantel, I would hang stockings, filled with nuts and candy canes. Around the cardboard hearth I placed empty boxes, wrapped in colorful paper and topped with curclicued bows made by the three lady salesclerks. Next came the plastic lighted 3-ft. Santa. Around the perimeter of the window I tacked strings of bubble lights, from which I draped tinfoil icicles. For my grand finale, I would write "samX yrreM" in spray snow on the inside of the plate glass window, so people driving by could read it properly.

It was, I suppose, rather tacky, but I was proud, and dad always told customers it was my work.

My father was diagnosed with cancer just before Christmas, 1964, but nobody told me it was terminal. I knew he had undergone surgery in a St. Louis hospital, that he had lost weight, his color was bad. But I was 13 and, as 13-year-olds do, assumed the worst was over and things would soon return to normal.

I was wrong. Throughout 1965, his cough grew worse, he grew weaker and thinner. My mother, who had never worked outside the house a day in her life, took over the operations of the store.

It was a tradition that on the Sunday before Christmas, Dad and I would go to a farm a mile south of town and chop down a cedar tree for our living room. But as Christmas 1965 grew nearer, there was no talk of a tree, decorations or of holiday plans.

One snowy night a few days before Christmas, I went to the farm, chopped down a tree, and dragged it home on my sled. When I called my mother out into the garage to see what I had brought home, she broke down weeping and told me there would be no Christmas because my father was going to die, and soon.

All I remember about that Christmas is the ambulance.

I know this column may seem inappropriate at this happy time of year, even ludicrous. Here I am, a grown man with his own wonderful family, bellyaching about something that happened 35 years ago. I know people who have experienced losses far more profound than mine. Death is part of life. I should have been able to get over it by now.

But losing a parent, as more and more of my middle-aged friends have found out lately, is something that's hard to get over. Losing a parent at Christmas when you're 14 is enough to take away the wonder and joy of the holiday forever.

I made my annual holiday shopping trip to the mall today. Carolers were singing "Auld Lang Syne," the song the townspeople sing at the end of *It's a Wonderful Life*, the movie that reminds me of my father. I had to leave the mall, go sit in my car, and beat up on myself for being such a wuss, for feeling so sad when everyone around me seems so joyful. I want to feel joyful too, but dammit, I can't.

And I'm not the only one. Mental health professionals report that millions of otherwise well-adjusted people plunge into funks at Christmastime. I bet a huge percentage of them lost loved ones at Christmas, the one time of year when everyone is supposed to be happy. For them, their wounds are ripped open anew every year the day after Thanksgiving and continue to bleed until New Year's Day when the tree is taken down and the decorations put away.

The rest of the year, I'm an upbeat kinda guy. But not at Christmas. And I want those of you who feel like me to know you're not alone and you're not crazy.

I understand how tough it is to keep a happy face when everyone is singing about merry gentlemen and triumph in the skies and all you really want for Christmas is something you can't have:

To be once again—for one blessed moment—a boy writing "samX yrreM" in spray snow on the window of your father's store, secure in the knowledge you'll actually have one.

Thank you for flying with us today

Last week I took flights on four airlines in two days. Each airline's in-flight magazine featured a letter from the C.E.O., touting all the wonderful things the airline was doing for me, its valued Customer. Every letter sounded just the same. Here's one.

Dear Passenger:

With airline mega-mergers, higher fuel prices, labor unrest and so-called "air rage" dominating the news, I would like to review with you important steps we at Reliable Air have implemented for your safety, comfort and convenience.

1. Additional legroom: I'm 5 ft. 7 in. myself so I know how uncomfortable it can be to sit in a cramped middle seat with not only your own but someone else's knees in your face. So here's welcome news. We've removed lavatories from our fleet. This has enabled us to add 2 inches of pitch between seats.

2. We hear you loud and clear. You're hungry: We admit it. We were wrong to discontinue in-flight meals. You'll be pleased to know our popular "StixFix" meal service—a Slim Jim, stick of Polly-O String Cheese and, for dessert, a luscious red Twizzler—has been reinstated in First Class on all flights of nine hours or more.

3. More timely announcements: Following the unfortunate incident in Detroit in which 300 Customers, understandably upset after a 72-hour delay during which no announcements were made, set fire to our Customer Service Desk and to three ramp agents, we quickly realized we must do a better job keeping you informed.

To facilitate communications, we are installing telephones between our headquarters and every airport to inform personnel of possible delays so they, in turn, can keep *you* posted.

4. Our fleet revitalization: Two years ago, the average age of our fleet was 27 years old. Today, it's a youthful 24, and I'm pleased to report we just signed leases on 12 "like-new" L-1011s, which will allow us to retire our aging 707s and Convair 880s. On our hourly LaGuardia–Boston Shuttle, we plan to replace Boeing 727s with a fleet of Chevrolet Suburbans, which hold more passengers than a typical 727 anyway and will complete the trip using 10 fewer gallons of fuel. Gate-to-gate travel time will be reduced by 30 minutes because Suburbans are not subject to air traffic control delays.

On order are technically-advanced new aircraft that will require only two people, rather than three, in the cockpit—a pilot and co-pilot. Better yet, we are in negotiations with our Pilots' Union to further reduce the number of pilots per plane to one-half per flight. This will require more frequent use of the autopilot, and that's good news for you, our valued Customer, because unlike human pilots, autopilots never make annoying announcements like "We are over the Grand Canyon" in the middle of the night when you can't see anyway.

5. Airline partnerships: Now that Reliable has formed marketing alliances with Air Afghanistan and Ugandair, you have more choices of destinations and more ways than ever to use your frequent flyer miles. Ugandair, for instance, has set aside several dozen seats for award travel during January 2006.

6. We are saving you money: Reliable was the first airline to require its pilots to taxi aircraft from the gate to the runway using just one engine. This resulted in annual fuel savings of $40,000,000, some of which we hope to pass on to you in the form of lower fares. As of January 1, Reliable became the first airline to not just taxi, but to actually *fly* scheduled flights using a single engine. After all, today's sophisticated twin-engine airliners can safely cruise through the skies on one Pratt & Whitney fanjet, saving you money.

7. More overhead space: You told us you are tired of having flight attendants confiscate your laptops, purses and infants as you board, informing you they will have to check them to your destination, because some low-life snuck on during the early boarding process and crammed three duffel bags, two suitcases, four shopping bags and a crate of live chickens into all the available overhead storage space. So we changed our carry-on policy. Starting March 1, each passenger will be limited to no more than one carry-on. (For your convenience and safety, the combined dimensions of your carry-on cannot exceed 10" x 10" x 2.")

8. More first class seats: We know you're frustrated with trying to exchange your frequent flyer miles for upgrades and being told none are available, only to find, when you board, that the First Class section is packed with Reliable employees going on vacation. Effective immediately, no more than 70% of the First Class seats on any given flight will be occupied by employees.

In conclusion, now that Reliable is merging with United, American, Delta, Continental, Southwest, Northwest, Midwest, Midway, Air Polynesia, TWA, ATA, TAP, SAS, JAL, KLM, Cubana, British Airways, Air France, El Al, Aeroflot and Air New Zealand (pending government approval), we will be able to offer even more frequent service to more destinations. You have my word that Reliable, as one of two surviving global airlines, and the only carrier serving cities east of the Rockies, will strive to not only make your travels affordable but as pleasant as possible.

Enjoy your flight today and thank you for flying Reliable, winner of the prestigious Powers award for the most convenient schedule of any airline serving airports in states with panhandles. We owe our success to Customers like you, and look forward to serving you for many years to come.

What colleges don't want you to know

My son and I spent part of his spring break visiting colleges he has applied to for the fall term.

If you have ever been the parent of a college-bound student, you know the routine.

It starts off with an "information session." An admissions officer presents an overview of the college. After that, parents and prospective students are divided into groups, to take campus tours led by fresh-faced student leaders.

I've taken seven or eight of these tours over the last year, and they're all the same. The student guide leads parents and their offspring—who look like they can't wait to get away from them—around campus, pointing out landmarks, classrooms, and a plaque or letter embedded in a sidewalk underclassmen *must not* step on lest they be cursed forever. They also visit a typical dormitory room, and stop in the cafeteria.

My favorite part of the tour are the questions anxious-looking parents ask the guides. These never vary. The guides always respond politely, regurgitating programmed answers meant to assuage parental anxiety. But I can tell they're not being 100% truthful.

Recently after one such tour of a major university, I ran into a guide in the student union. I offered to buy him a Mountain Dew if he would tell me the truth. He agreed . . . on the condition I wouldn't mention his name or college.

Here, according to him, are the questions parents ask most frequently **(Q)** . . . the answers the college has trained him to give **(A)** . . . and the truthful answers **(T)** he would provide if the admissions office wouldn't take away his scholarship.

Q: *I've read that binge drinking is more rampant on college campuses today than ever before. Are there organized alcohol-free activities?*

A: Absolutely. There's a sizable organization of students who know they don't need alcohol to enjoy social activities. Last month, for instance, this group spent a fun-filled day at Six Flags and organized an all-night Disney Film Festival. They are also very active in the Community Gardens project, where they raise herbs for shut-ins.

T: The organization is called STROML—Students to Repeal Oppressive Marijuana Laws.

Q: *How safe is it for my daughter to walk back to her dorm late at night after an evening at the library?*

A: Notice there are streetlights everywhere, as well as call boxes that provide instant connection to campus security, local and state police and the FBI. In addition, your daughter can call Safe Rides from anywhere on campus and will be driven to her dorm in a Brink's truck by a former Green Beret and WWF champion.

T: Like most freshman girls who are thrilled to be away from their overprotective parents, she'll probably spend most nights in her boyfriend's room anyway, so it's no big deal.

Q: *Does the cafeteria serve balanced meals?*

A: Breakfast typically includes a choice of cereals, whole grain breads and fruit. Lunch and dinner is a broth-based soup or salad course, grilled fish or chicken and a vegetable medley.

T: In the basement directly beneath the cafeteria is a food court with a Burger King, Dunkin' Donuts, KFC, Ben & Jerry's, Pizza Hut and Godiva Factory Outlet where student meal tickets are welcome.

Q: *Where can my child go for help with term papers?*

A: At our Writing Center, students can submit drafts of papers to graduate students from the English Department, who will be happy to point out errors in spelling, grammar, logic and syntax.

T: If your kid wants his paper shaped into an "A," it'll cost $50, a "B" is $40, and a "C" is $25.

Q: *Should my child bring a computer from home?*

A: If desired, but there's no need—we have four computer labs that are open 24 hours a day.

T: Unfortunately, all four computers are fully booked until 2006.

Q: *Where do most of the kids on this campus come from?*

A: We pride ourselves on the diversity of our student population. Approximately 60 percent are from states east of the Mississippi, 30 percent from west of the Mississippi, and the rest are from foreign countries.

T: Of those from the east, approximately 97 percent are rich white kids from Connecticut, mostly Fairfield County.

Q: *Are fraternities and sororities active on campus?*

A: No. The university shut down the Greek system following an unfortunate incident in which the Iota Eta Theta house burned down when a group of pledges scrubbed the floors with grain alcohol during Hell Week and an untended candle fell to the floor.

T: Now that they're all underground, virtually 100 percent of our student body belongs to one.

Q: *What percentage of students are admitted on an "early decision" basis, in which the school informs them they have been admitted months before the general admissions process closes?*

A: Less than 10 percent.

T: Only those whose parents attach to their application a check large enough to build a new wing on our library.

Q: *Are you glad you chose this school?*

A: Oh yes. Although I was accepted at Harvard, Yale and Oxford, I chose (college name deleted) because of its superior academics, outstanding athletic program and the beauty of the campus.

T: Do you think I'd be answering stupid questions like this if my parole officer didn't require me to work my way through college by leading neurotic parents like you around?

Paula's amazing garlic pickle diet

When: Between 8 p.m. and 1 a.m. New Year's Eve.

Where: Continental Airlines flight 4901 from Aruba, a fully-loaded DC-10 running 24 hours late due to Saturday's snowstorm, a flight whose passengers would observe the beginning of the New Year on the ground at Newark during a 1-hour wait for a gate, and who would wait until 3 a.m. for their luggage to be offloaded.

The Soliloquist: A 50ish woman three rows behind me with a voice that could shatter glass.

Wanna listen in? Fifty passengers within earshot had no choice for five nonstop hours. You, mercifully, can turn the page.

"I didn't gain an ounce—I swear to God, not one ounce—on the cruise and I ate five meals a day for seven days. It's the pickles, I swear to God. I tried and tried to lose weight—how the hell do I turn on this light? I can't see a damned thing—then my neighbor Paula told me about the pickle diet. Did that steward say the movie is *Matrix*? I saw that at the new multiplex in Garden City, it didn't make any sense so we got up and walked after an hour…

"I even ate two breakfasts every morning. I'd get up at 7 and go to the dining room and order off the menu, then when Norman would get up around 10 we'd go through the top deck buffet and I'd have another cup of coffee and a bagel. Did you try those scrambled eggs? Fabulous! Some things taste better when you make them in quantity and scrambled eggs are definitely better the more of them you cook at one time…

"Paula said that if you eat a big garlic pickle a half hour before every meal that you can eat whatever you want, as much as you want, and you won't gain weight. What'd he say? Oh, *The Patriot*, not *Matrix*. Oh yeah, we saw that last summer, or was it last spring? No, I remember now, it was right after Fourth of July 'cause we were up at the lake with Larry and Sheila and we'd talked about going to see it then but we didn't because Sheila's sister had a heart attack and she went to the hospital to be with her, so we closed up the cottage and came home…

"Mel Gibson, is that not the most gorgeous man you ever saw? I don't care if he is having to dye his hair these days and has—what is it?—10 or 12 kids, that man is beauty-ful, that's the word for him. *Four dollars* for a headset? I'm not gonna pay $4 for a movie I already saw, I'd rather sit here and chat with you. I wonder what that man up there is writing on that pad? Looks like he's working. You'd think people would be able to take a vacation and leave work behind but I guess some people just don't know how to relax . . .

"Anyway, I started eating a garlic pickle every day before lunch and dinner—I never eat breakfast except when I go on a cruise which we've done every Christmas for, I guess, 10 years now. Last year we took the *Fascination* but the *Horizon* was much nicer, a better class of people. There was money on that boat, I tell you. And the food—100 times better! My favorite part was seeing St. Kitts, we'd never been there even though we've visited 14 Caribbean islands if you count Cozumel in Mexico but nobody thinks of Cozumel as a Caribbean island . . .

"I lost 50 pounds, I swear to God, in six months. Just melted off, I didn't do anything different except eat that pickle twice a day. What? Oh yeah, it stinks, but let me tell you, I gargle with Lavoris right afterwards and garlic pickles and Lavoris don't mix at all. Who wants to eat a big meal after you've eaten a garlic pickle and gargled with cinnamon mouthwash?

"Look up front, what are they serving? It smells good, and check that out—real plates and little tablecloths for the tray tables. Someday before I die, I swear to God, I'm gonna spring for First Class. I wanna know what it feels like to have people falling all over themselves to be nice instead of being treated like pond scum here in the back of the bus and getting this garbage. A pita wrap sandwich, did you ever hear of eating a pita wrap on New Year's Eve?

"And did you hear that snippy stewardess tell me the bar is closed? No, you were in the bathroom, you couldn't have heard it, but all I wanted was a Diet Coke. Is that too much to ask from an airline that left us stranded for 24 hours and didn't even apologize? I know they couldn't do anything about the weather for God's sake, but a Diet Coke isn't too much to ask for, is it? We'll probably be circling Newark at midnight. Some party we'll be making back here! I bet they get Champagne up front, but here in the back of the bus they won't even give me a Diet Coke . . .

"So I ate a big pickle before every meal, but after six months it quit working. Listen to me here, I hit a stone wall. I didn't gain weight but I didn't lose any either. So Paula told me the same thing happened to her, but she kept eating those garlic pickles and two months later she started losing again. And so did I. I want to lose 50 more pounds this year, that's my resolution . . .

"A salesgirl in a shop in Aruba—I was trying on a dress—was heavyset like me. She told me I looked good in the dress, and I told her about Paula's garlic pickle diet, but she'd never heard of a garlic pickle, I wonder why? Maybe they don't have them in Aruba, but I can't imagine that. Of all the islands we've visited Aruba's one of the most advanced and besides, what kind of civilized country wouldn't have garlic pickles?"

A *Survivor's* guide to a family reunion

Are you watching *Survivor*, the hottest TV show of the summer?

If not, here's the premise. CBS has taken 16 people with nothing in common, and dropped them off in some Godforsaken spot. The castaways have to figure out how to get along with one another and, each week, vote one of their fellow survivors off in a "tribal council" meeting in which the expelled member's torch is dramatically extinguished.

Viewers get to see them eating repulsive meals, wearing revealing clothes (even those who shouldn't), bickering endlessly, complaining behind each others' backs, forming alliances with other castaways, and competing in inane games.

In short, it resembles nothing more than a typical reunion of the Dryden clan.

I received an e-mail from cousin Harold last week announcing plans for our next family reunion. He gave a choice of three options and asked us all to vote.

Option A: We can pitch tents on what was once my grandparents' farm in Missouri—known affectionately as "the old home place"—where the swimming pond is swarming with copperheads.

Option B: We can rent adjacent timeshare condos in Gatlinburg, Tennessee, which, Harold has figured out, is within 100 miles of the epicenter of where my grandparents' 107 descendants are living. One afternoon, we can all visit Dollywood.

Option C: We can take a three-day Carnival Cruise from Miami to the Bahamas for which Harold's sixth wife, a travel agent, can arrange group rates and cabin upgrades. Of all the options, that's my worst nightmare—being trapped on a "Fun Ship" surrounded by drunken revelers, half of whom I am related to, while hearing Kathie Lee's "Ain't We Got Fun" piped in over the PA system.

I personally would vote for Option D, which wasn't offered: Let's assemble on the grounds of the Missouri State Penitentiary where cousin Forest might be able to look out from his cell while we play volleyball. After all, it's the final reunion we'll have in his lifetime unless the Governor changes his mind at the last minute.

My family sure is a strange bunch.

Like the cast of *Survivor*, which includes people as diverse as a retired Navy SEAL, a neurologist, a trucker and a newly-minted Ivy League graduate, my relatives represent many professions.

There's everything from a shrink (my niece, who became one, she says, because of the dysfunctional family in which she was raised), to cousin Gilbert, a Ph.D. who lives in Guam, where he is recognized as a leading authority on the mating habits of shrews. In addition, there's a plumber, retired Army general, CIA agent, FedEx pilot, math professor, pharmacist, linoleum installer, an assistant manager of a Wendy's and, to our eternal shame, several lawyers.

We range in age from 87 (my mother) to four (my great-niece).

Though we all inherited the blue eyes and pale albino-like skin of our northern European ancestors, which turns the color of raw yellow fin tuna after a half-hour of exposure to sunlight, we have adorned ourselves with lots of body art, just like the castaways on *Survivor.*

My youngest niece, a student at a Seven Sisters college, has a belly-button ring.

My cousin Edwin the actor (appearing on stage this summer in Omaha as Troilus in *Troilus & Cressida, the Musical*), has an ear studded with six diamonds, not to mention a studded tongue which made him exceedingly difficult to understand when we last saw him perform.

I am sporting at the end of my nose my annual too-much-fun-in-the-sun summer zit the size of a ripe tomato, to which I'm applying Adult-Strength Clearasil by the gallon.

We represent divergent political points-of-view. Cousin Tim's wife was Elizabeth Dole's personal assistant. My sister was active in Jesse Jackson's presidential campaign.

Like the maggots and rats they eat on *Survivor,* disgusting food is an important tradition of every reunion. In our family, a "covered" dish means covered with Velveeta. It pops up in everything, from Cousin Juanita's braunschweiger-stuffed deviled eggs to Aunt Opal's 7-layer congealed salad. At least those dishes are vaguely edible.

But I'd rather eat scalloped rats in Velveeta than Aunt Betty's Devils Food Zucchini Cake. She makes 10 at a time to get rid of the surplus zucchini she grows in her garden, and keeps them in the freezer for special occasions.

I'll be honest. I really dread going to the reunion. Don't you dread going to yours?

Of course you do. So here's a concept inspired by *Survivor* I'm going to propose when we gather. Maybe you should bring it up at your next reunion, too.

I'm going to propose that, every three hours, we assemble in a tribal council and vote one ultra-obnoxious member out of the family by secret ballot.

We'll take away their coat of arms, and send them packing.

For example, Aunt Jewel, the fundamentalist who, whenever

she sees me frying catfish on the cast iron grill, starts quoting scripture about how the Lord will provide. "If you repeat that loaves and fishes story one more time, I'm going to vote you out." That should shut her trap.

Or, when cousin Darlene, as she does every year, insists we all watch a video of her handbell choir's most recent Easter performance. "You ding-dong, you're outta here."

John is complaining again about how Uncle Ralph shafted him in his will? Hand over your torch.

And if, for some reason, any of the castouts refuse to leave, I know someone who will gladly go in their place.

It's the least I can do.

After all, we're family.

And the final *Jeopardy!* answer is....

I can't add or subtract, have trouble remembering what grades my kids are in, and sometimes get lost driving to my office.

But ask me to name the capital of Mozambique, the vice presidents of the U.S., in order, or the number of gold medals the U.S. won in the 1936 Berlin Olympics, and I'll rattle the answers off instantly. I've always had a head for useless information.

And that's why I'm obsessed with online *Jeopardy!*. Every night, I log on to jeopardy.com and spend hours going head-to-head with strangers who also have trivial minds, not to mention the social lives of Benedictine monks.

I've been a *Jeopardy!* fanatic since the '60s, when the original version, hosted by Art Fleming, debuted. I wrote away to become a contestant but was informed smart-ass 11-year-olds weren't welcome.

In 1985, when *Jeopardy!* in its second incarnation, hosted by Alex Trebek, began, I applied immediately, and was invited to tryouts in New Haven. I arrived to find an auditorium packed with 300 intellectual-types—mostly Yalies and professors. I figured I was doomed. But I was one of only 12 who passed the 55-question multiple-choice test, and was asked to stay for a mock game. I did well on that, smiling often to demonstrate my outgoing personality the contestant coordinator said was key, and was told to expect a call.

When the call arrived, inviting me to Hollywood, I was over the moon.

We had a two-year-old at the time, and my wife was expecting our second child, so it was decided I'd go to L.A. by myself.

At dinner the night before I left, our son, in his highchair, started wailing about something. To make him laugh, I picked up a toy clown with a suction cup on the bottom . . . stuck it in the middle of my forehead . . . and began moving my head in circles, making the clown bob up and down. My son shut up, and I finished dinner in peace with a plastic clown protruding from my forehead.

When I removed it, the suction had produced a perfectly round 3-inch purple hickey in the center of my forehead. All night long my wife kept shining a flashlight in my face to see if it was fading. It wasn't. It was getting darker, as bruises do.

The next day she bought a flesh-colored makeup called "Erase" that's supposed to hide anything, and applied a thick layer over the hickey. It was still visible, but much less obvious.

That afternoon I flew to L.A. where, the moment I stepped out of the terminal and into the heat, the makeup began running into my eyes, blinding me.

The next day, I smeared more Erase over the hickey, and presented myself at the Sony Studios, along with a dozen other contestants.

A week's worth of *Jeopardy!*—five episodes—is taped in one afternoon. I was selected to appear on the first show and instructed to report to makeup. The makeup man was fascinated by my hickey which, by now, was almost black, and called Alex over to see it. I told Alex how I got it. He thought the story was hilarious, and asked if we could talk about it during the "interview" portion of the show we were about to tape. I said "no."

I don't think Alex liked me much after that.

The reigning champion was a man in his 60s, a retired teacher. The other challenger was a woman my age.

The categories for Round 1 couldn't have been worse, and included The Gay '90s, Mythology, Weather and Mammals.

By the end of the round, I was in negative territory, sweating profusely under the hot lights. During the commercial break, the makeup man barely had to touch up Alex and the other contestants. He used a trowel to apply Erase to my forehead.

However, as low scorer, I got to select the first answer in Double Jeopardy, where I swept the Business & Industry category, racking up $3,000. By the end of Double Jeopardy, I had $6,700, the champion had $5,000, the other challenger $1,700.

The final category was "Pop Music."

I bet $5,000, assuming the champion would wager it all, feeling confident because I was younger and hipper.

The final *Jeopardy!* answer? Here it is, verbatim. *"Written as Moritat, this song has appeared in the Billboard Top 40 longer and more often than any other song."*

The damned *Jeopardy!* theme song—dum dum dum dum, dum dum dum…dum dum dum dum dum, dumdumdumdumdum—started playing. It was the longest 30 seconds of my life.

I hadn't a clue. I wrote, "What is _____?"

The other challenger, also clueless, bet her entire wad, and finished with zero. But the champion knew, and finished first with $10,000. As second-place finisher, I won a La-Z Boy chair, Dynasty carpeting and a lifetime supply of Fleischmann's Yeast.

I sat in the audience for the next four tapings. Naturally, I knew everything—the categories were right up my alley—and would have buzzed in much faster than the slowpokes on stage. I would have been a five-time champion, and been invited back for the Tournament of Champions.

And, if I had invested all the money I would have surely won back in '85 in Microsoft or Walmart, I'd be rich and living in Tahiti (capital, Papeete), spending my days getting backrubs from women in grass skirts.

Instead, I have to work like a dog to pay the bills and come home at night and play *Jeopardy!* online until midnight with people who, for all I know, are serial killers. No applause. No money. No glory. Pathetic when you think about it.

And oh, if you're wondering the correct question I should have posed to the final *Jeopardy!* answer, here's my reply.

What is, "If you're so smart, why don't you figure it out?"

Clip this column and stash it in a drawer

Take this quiz. Be honest.

Your side of the bathroom countertop you share with your spouse looks like a:

A. Kohler showroom display.
B. Sunoco men's room.

Before you leave work each evening, you:

A. Clear any unfinished paperwork from your desk by placing it in file folders, the trash can, your "out" box or on someone else's desk

B. Tape a "do not enter" sign to your office door so the cleaning crew won't disturb the piles of paper on your desk, credenza, chairs and floor.

If strangers were to look into your dresser drawers, they would:

A. Be impressed by the way you've cleverly organized your socks and underwear.

B. Find hundreds of yellowed newspaper clippings, a box of chocolates from Valentine's Day 1989, and a tipped-over container of cremated dog remains.

If you answered "A" to two or more of the above, you're pathologically neat, like 50% of the people I know.

If you answered "B," you can come sit by me, soon as I clear all these magazines off the sofa. You're my kinda slob.

Of all the issues that divide our society, the ongoing battle between neat people and those of us who are order-challenged—a term I much prefer to "pig," which my wife calls me often—is perhaps the most insurmountable.

Naturally, neat freaks almost always attract order-challenged individuals as spouses and friends, and vice-versa.

Like most writers I know—OK, every writer I know—I keep hundreds of scraps of paper on which I jot down ideas as they occur to me.

For instance, I write most of my columns on paper scraps I keep stashed in my car, because I'm often struck by inspiration as I drive to and from my office.

I then leave these scraps on the dashboard, console, back seat and floor. I drive a convertible, but I never lower the top because everything will blow away.

The computer has revolutionized the lives of writers like me, because work in progress that used to be kept on paper can now be stored on hard drives. But experts now tell us we're supposed to keep computer files neat and tidy, too. I was recently notified by our computer systems guru at work that I needed to delete 6,000 files and e-mails ASAP, because they were clogging the server, making it impossible for others in the office to conduct business.

I had to spend a half-day deleting files—which I resented mightily—and, of course, printed out several hundred, in case I need them someday. The hard copies now rest on the floor under my desk, along with tax returns dating back to the '70s.

I once stopped by to see a fanatically-neat friend and found him painting the underside of his closet shelves. "Why bother?" I asked. "Only a dachshund or one of the surviving Munchkins would know they're bare wood."

"But I'd know," he said solemnly, as if I—who haven't been able to shut my closet door for years because of all the stuff crammed into it, including the size 38 slim suit with bell-bottom trousers I wore to my first job interview—could relate. Fat chance.

I have a theory that obsessive orderliness is a sign of a mind that is anything but. We all know people who brag, "I find it relaxing to scrub bathroom floors" or "I stayed up all night cleaning the garage" as if they deserve the Good Housekeeping Seal of Approval. If you ask me, they're nuts.

Nevertheless, I must admit that some of the people I admire most keep their homes, including their basements, neat as a pin, and that some of the most productive employees in my company keep their offices immaculate. Mine, on the other hand, has a stray cat in it, along with a litter box.

I've always been this way. When I was an SAE pledge in college, it was an old fraternity tradition that the pledges would leave without warning for a long weekend and go to New Orleans. It was also tradition that active members would break into pledges' rooms while they were gone and trash them.

My roommate and I returned to find overturned ashtrays, a 10-lb. bag of sugar, mildew-covered towels, reams of paper and several dozen half-empty cans of Busch Bavarian strewn across our room, exactly as we'd left it. Every active who entered to trash it thought someone else already had.

My wife complains bitterly about the books I buy continually, which long ago filled the bookcases we had custom-built in three rooms. We even added a room specifically for my books, but it was stacked to the rafters in less than a year.

I always keep several dozen books stacked along my side of

the bed. I maintain that the time I spend reading is more productive than the time I would spend placing them neatly on shelves where I'd never be able to find them when I need them. I've read almost all of them and those I haven't I'll get around to someday.

One thing I know for sure. When the Grim Reaper comes to take me away, I won't regret for a moment the time I didn't spend straightening up or painting the insides of closets. But I'll sure be happy I read all those books.

And who knows? Maybe he won't be able to find me, hidden underneath them all.

If you want to see them do their thing...

With the exception of last week's Lieberman-Cheney debate, in which the two vice-presidential contenders actually *answered* the questions the moderator posed, most political debates are farcical. They're not debates at all, because the candidates are allowed to say anything they want, and aren't held accountable for failing to answer inconvenient questions that get in the way of their self-serving sound bites.

Like the Chatty Cathy dolls of the '60s that were programmed by Hasbro, Kenner or whatever toy manufacturer made them to recite phrases like "I wuv you," most political candidates have a repertoire of seven or eight statements that have been programmed into them by their media advisors. When asked a question, they recite one of these programmed statements as answers, as if someone was standing behind them, pulling a string.

How many times in the first presidential "debate" did Gore remind us that Social Security "should be put in a lockbox?" Six? Eight? How many times did Bush call Gore's spending proposals "fuzzy math?" These responses were never answers to the moderator's questions, merely programmed sound bites, just like Chatty Cathy's.

Want proof candidates are being programmed? I've gotten my hands on a transcript of a debate that took place recently between two candidates for Senate in a state somewhere west of the Hudson. Here it is.

Moderator

Candidate A, you once characterized Candidate B as, quote, "a fool with the IQ of a gnat who inherited his money, name and political brand name." If given the opportunity, would you choose to take back this characterization?

Candidate A

Choose is the operative word. I believe women have the right to choose. They can choose BMWs, Cadillacs, Mercedes, any make and model they want under my plan because there will be such a huge Social Security surplus we'll have to start paying *extremely large benefits* to people at age 35.

Moderator

Candidate B, would you care to respond?

Candidate B

Fuzzy Wuzzy was a bear, Fuzzy Wuzzy is an heir.

Moderator

Candidate B, your opponent once said on the *Today Show* that, quote, "Bill Clinton's marriage is so strong, I can't imagine him even *looking* at another woman, much less engaging in lascivious conduct in the Oval Office." Do you believe he owes the American people an apology?

Candidate B

Fuzzy Wuzzy was a bear, perhaps Bill's wife's a Frigidaire.

Moderator

And what would you say about that Candidate A?

Candidate A

In the studio audience tonight is a Social Security recipient who had to pump one of those railroad flatcars like the ones in old Mickey Mouse cartoons all the way from Seattle to be here. Under my proposal, with all the Social Security money she will get, not only will she be able to fly first class she will get *double frequent flyer* miles.

Moderator

Do you agree, Candidate B?

Candidate B

Fuzzy Wuzzy was a bear, Fuzzy loves to fly through air.

Moderator

Candidate B, you've repeatedly attacked the music industry for contributing to the decline of America's youth. Your opponent, on the other hand, has accepted more than $10 million in contributions from artists such as rapper Eminem whose music advocates violence and drug use. What would you say to that?

Candidate B

Fuzzy Wuzzy was a bear. Fuzzy wants some cash from Cher.

Moderator

Candidate A, today's debate marks only the second time you've visited this state, and the first time was when your plane had to make an emergency landing. Given your unfamiliarity with it, how do you think you can effectively represent its interests in Washington?

Candidate A

My mother took a train through this state once, en route to Washington to watch FDR sign the original Social Security Bill. My newest proposal is an improvement on FDR's, because it guarantees every recipient dinner once a week at a Morton's Steak House—tax, tip and wine included.

Moderator

Your response, Candidate B.

Candidate B

Fuzzy Wuzzy was a bear, Fuzzy likes his medium-rare.

Moderator

Candidate A, a leading women's group recently likened you to, and I quote, "A sanctimonious supercilious schoolmarm who claims to have invented the slicing machine for Wonder Bread when, in fact, it was actually invented 35 years before you were born." How would you reply?

Candidate A

As I said in the Declaration of Independence when I drafted it, Social Security and my opponent—who, as you can see, is frantically changing the batteries on his pager so his advisors can send him text answers to the questions he is so deftly ignoring—belong in a lockbox.

Moderator

Your response?

Candidate B (reading from pager)

You idiot, you're supposed to be saying fuzzy *thinking*, not Fuzzy *Wuzzy*. Remember the answers we rehearsed and take three deep breaths before you reply.

Candidate A

See what I mean? As I was saying, Social Security is…

Moderator

I'm sorry, we're out of time. Thank you Candidates A and B, and thank you all for watching.

Sure you can buy my vote

I was born during the waning days of Harry Truman's administration. The next president will be the 11th of my lifetime.

Ideally, he will possess the best traits of all the presidents under whom I've lived. He will have the common sense of Truman, the military know-how of Ike, and the personal style of JFK. He will share LBJ's commitment to human rights, Nixon's diplomacy skills, Ford's fundamental decency and Carter's compassion. He will be a great communicator like Reagan, have the grace of Bush, and the hair stylist of Clinton.

The night before the election, the next president will purchase a 30-minute spot on TV for a live speech in which he makes the following promises. He will be elected in a landslide. The day after his inauguration, Congress, wisely interpreting the public's response as a mandate, will enact enabling legislation so he can carry out his pledges.

Here are excerpts from the speech the next president will give if he wants my vote.

"People who have liposuction and other elective cosmetic surgery will receive tax credits for beautifying America."

"America is a melting pot and that's what makes this such an interesting place. Nevertheless, I will not pander by appointing a fixed percentage of men, women, African-Americans, Hispanics, Asians, gays and lesbians, one-armed individuals of Icelandic extraction or whatever to positions of responsibility. Anyone in their right mind wants only the best for their country. That's why I will appoint the best-qualified persons. Most of them will not be professional politicians."

" 'Pick 6' lottery games will be outlawed, so people wishing to make purchases in convenience stores and gas stations won't have to wait 20 minutes while some moron who should be spending money on food or education for his family chooses every possible combination of numbers."

"The Lincoln bedroom will be occupied only by visiting heads of state and, of course, by my mother when she visits the White House."

"It would be nice if Americans could use guns wisely but they clearly can't—not when first-graders are shooting each other. I will therefore propose the following Constitutional amendment: All privately-owned guns will be kept in guarded arsenals. Those who claim they need guns to hunt because they are hungry will be given vouchers they can take to supermarkets for food. In the event of enemy invasion, guns will be returned to their original owners."

"There must be at least one foot of legroom between seats in all commercial airliners. This is for safety as well as comfort."

"It's not my fault millions of farmers are raising crops they can't sell at a profit. We don't pay subsidies to artists or columnists who can't sell their work for the price they want. Why pay them to farmers?"

"Since they clearly have money to burn, those who insist on driving gas-guzzling SUVs will have to pay a 100% surtax on the purchase price. Current SUV owners will be required to attend special truck-driving schools, where they will learn how to keep their vehicles under control and to use common courtesy."

"It will be illegal to use cell phones in moving motor vehicles or within earshot of anyone else."

"People who breed more than one litter of dogs or cats for

profit per year will be forced to ride in a cage in the back of an unheated truck for days at a time, and will be confined to a room no larger than 3 ft. x 3 ft. for up to 6 months."

"If a woman wants to end a pregnancy, she has to decide if she's willing to take the risk that she may some day have to explain her decision to a wrathful God. But the government doesn't have the right to decide she can't have an abortion. Please remember that our Constitution, unlike that of Iran and other wacko nations, guarantees separation of church and state."

"The base salary for teachers will be raised to $100,000 effective immediately for those who pass a test demonstrating proficiency in their specialty. They will receive $10,000 annual raises thereafter. Funding for this initiative will come from reallocating the money federal, state and local governments are wasting on anti-smoking commercials. People who don't know by now that smoking is bad aren't listening to them."

"Anyone who brings a lawsuit and loses in court will be required to pay court costs and legal fees of the party they were suing. That should unclog our courts of whining losers trying to make a fast buck."

"Insurance companies will henceforth allow pharmacists to dispense more than a month's supply of pills to people who have prescriptions that need to be refilled regularly. If that person dies, his or her estate will be required to return unused pills."

"Tax deductions for individuals will be disallowed because they are unfair. Instead, there will be one flat tax of 15% or so imposed on all earned or unearned income. This will result in more money to help the disadvantaged among us."

"My spouse will not run for any public office while I am serving as president, it's undignified."

"In conclusion, I have no siblings who will embarrass the nation by lending their name to beer brands or trying to be rock stars."

"Thank you, and good night."

I'm letting Clyde decide

On Tuesday November 7, I'm letting Clyde decide who I should vote for.

Clyde, as regular readers know, is my family's lovable but dumb-as-a-stone miniature dachshund.

"Ha-ha," you say. But I'm not joking. I'm dead serious. I take my country's future very seriously. Too bad the party leaders who allowed Gore and Bush to run in the first place don't.

When my alarm goes off that morning, the thought of having to cast my vote for either of them will make me want to push the "snooze" button on my alarm clock and go back to bed for four more years.

I've been unenthusiastic about Gore and Bush from the get-go. I have a thing against brand-name politicians who, if their last names weren't the same as their famous fathers', would probably be selling insurance somewhere.

Nevertheless, I've tried to stay up to date, so I could make an informed decision when the time came. I watched both conventions. Tuned into all three debates. Read editorial after editorial, article after article, watched the Sunday morning political talk shows, anything and everything I could possibly do.

My problem with Gore and Bush is with them personally. Specifically, with how they present themselves. A president has to not only be capable, he or she has to project an image of leadership, of trust. Neither do.

In real life, as writers have editorialized endlessly, Gore has the personality of a turkey sandwich on Wonder Bread and has had to work extra hard to come across as likable. He hasn't succeeded.

He reminds me of a know-it-all schoolboy who sits on the front row, smugly raising his hand in answer to every question and thrusting it repeatedly in the air to get the teacher's attention, becoming angry when she recognizes someone else. Why? Because he knows he's right, everyone else is wrong.

Ever notice how, when he's talking about taxes going up, he lifts his hand? I do that with Clyde when I want him to jump. When he talks about tax decreases, he lowers his hand as if to say "down boy," just as I do to Clyde when I come home in a nice suit and he jumps all over me.

Why the hand signals? Because Al thinks that we, who didn't go to Harvard like he did, don't know what up or down means, so he has to show us. His high-paid advisors don't tell him to make those patronizing gestures. I imagine they're telling him not to. But he can't help himself, it's bred into him—just like it's bred into Clyde to dig for moles—that we're all idiots who need him to explain things to us because we don't u-n-d-e-r-s-t-a-n-d.

Hate to tell you Al, but we do understand. And what I have come to understand is that you are so obnoxious I don't think I can stand to see you on TV every night for the next four years.

Bush, on the other hand, watches Gore's hand movements intently when they're together, because he's probably learning something. Dubya comes across exactly as what former Texas governor Anne Richards claimed his father was: A kid born with a "silver foot in his mouth."

Unlike Gore, Bush seems to be an affable, easygoing kinda guy. But as much as you might like to raise a pint with him at the country club bar, he's not exactly the sharpest tool in the shed.

He seems to have little control over the facts and has no real plan other than pandering to the ultra-rich, ultra-conservative backward-leaning wackos who control the Republican party at the national level.

Whatever they tell him to do, he'll do if it will help him get elected. Those who support him rationalize that we needn't worry because, if he wins, he will surround himself with advisors who have triple digit IQs. But in the meantime, how many times are we going to embarrassed watching him stumble over facts and confusing Sheboygan with Chechyna?

Come to think of it, how come his father isn't campaigning for him? Does Senior know something we don't?

Clyde and I watched the first debate and, after that, I decided I was definitely voting for Gore, grating though I found his performance. Actually, I wasn't going to vote for Gore so much as I was voting against Bush, who clearly didn't have a grasp of the issues like Gore did, much less a plan.

After the second debate, in which Dubya did somewhat better and Al was once again his condescending self, I decided to make up my mind after the third debate.

Following that debate, in which Al was particularly boorish, ignoring the rules and using hand signals for everything—I half expected him to break into the "Eensy Weensy Spider" to demonstrate his Social Security funding plan—I decided to vote for Bush. Rather, to vote against Gore.

Then, a few days later a friend sent an e-mail containing a couple of dozen Bush misstatements like, "For NASA, space is still a high priority" and, "If we don't succeed, we run the risk of failure." Déjà vu Dan "Mr. Potatoe-head" Quayle, my least-favorite political figure of modern times.

I can't vote for someone who's going to be the butt of Jay Leno's jokes for the next four years.

So I'm letting Clyde decide. Every morning after he eats, he jumps on the sofa and, by the time I leave for work, is fast asleep. Half the time he's on his back, with all four stubby legs pointing straight up in the air like a dead horse. Other times he's on his stomach, his long nose resting on his paws.

If Clyde's on his back when I leave for the polls, I'm voting for Gore. If he's on his stomach, it's Bush.

And if you, like me, are still undecided, call me that morning. I'll let you know which one of these dogs Clyde is recommending.

It's all Clyde's fault

Our nation is in Electoral Hell, and it's all Clyde's fault.

Clyde is my family's sweet but simple-minded miniature dachshund.

In my October 26th column entitled "I'm Letting Clyde Decide," I revealed that, like millions of voters who thought America deserved better than Gore or Bush, I was having trouble deciding which candidate was the least objectionable. I said I was going to let Clyde decide how I would vote.

Every morning, exhausted after the excitement of breakfast which sends him into a frenzy of tail-chasing, Clyde jumps on the sofa and falls into a deep sleep. I wrote that if, on Election Day, Clyde fell asleep on his back, as he does half the time, I would vote for Gore. If he fell asleep Sphinx-like on his stomach, as he does the rest of the time, I would cast my ballot for Bush.

He did neither. This is a complicated story with bizarre twists and turns, so bear with me here.

I send e-mail copies of every column I write to several dozen friends and family members scattered from Boston to Seattle. Many of them, in turn, forward it to others on their e-mail lists. I have no clue how many people actually receive and read *Doubting Thomas.* I was astonished once to receive e-mail from an SUV-loathing reader in New Zealand.

As usual, I e-mailed my "Clyde Decide" column to my friend Ted who lives in—get this—Palm Beach County, Florida. That county, as the world knows by now, is home of the infamous "butterfly" ballot on which the candidates' names were arranged with Reform Party candidate Pat Buchanan's name smack-dab between Bush and Gore.

At 7 a.m. on Election Day, I checked my e-mail. Ted had written, asking, "Which one of these dogs is Clyde recommending?"

I went into the other room to check. Clyde was snoring blissfully . . . *on his side.* In the four years he has lived with us, he has never—but never—slept on his side. I called my wife and kids in to see it. Like me, they were flabbergasted.

"He's on his side!" I e-mailed back. "Guess that means a vote for Buchanan."

I then forgot about it, and went out to vote, making up my mind on the way to the polls. (Note: I didn't vote for Buchanan. I may be strange but I'm not crazy.)

Ted, however, forwarded my e-mail reply to everyone on his list to whom he had sent the "Clyde Decide" column—around 30 people, many of them co-workers and neighbors in Palm Beach County.

Many of them, in turn, forwarded it to friends and family on *their* e-mail lists. Nobody has been able to determine the exact number of Palm Beach voters who received Clyde's recommendation.

That evening, when it became clear that the Florida returns were too close to call, many voters in Palm Beach County—a substantial percentage of them elderly—came forward to say they were confused by the butterfly ballot. They claimed they had accidentally voted for Pat Buchanan when, in fact, they meant to vote for Gore. (Personally, I don't understand it. These people can play seven or eight Bingo cards at one time, but they can't read a butterfly ballot?)

But here's the story you haven't heard. Hundreds of other

Palm Beach County voters have come forward alleging that, because of Clyde's recommendation, they meant to vote for *Buchanan* but may have inadvertently voted for *Gore.*

Gore campaign manager William "I Never Met An Election My Family Can't Throw To The Democrats" Daley is working hard to suppress this peculiar story and to obtain a gag order on those who claim they intended to vote for Clyde's man Buchanan but, confused by the ballot layout, voted for Gore instead.

Bush's people have been calling ten times a day, offering to send a Lear jet so Clyde can fly to Austin for a press conference with Bush and Cheney. At that event, the Bush people will claim that, for every Gore supporter who accidentally voted for Buchanan, there is another voter who, at Clyde's recommendation, intended to vote for Buchanan but accidentally voted for Gore.

It's a mess. And our nation's future hinges on the outcome.

Will we be led by Bush, who lost the popular vote, but may have won the Electoral College? If so, he will have a Republican Congress through which to push his conservative agenda and many claim he will appoint right-wingers to the Supreme Court. That will be Clyde's fault.

Or will the election go to Gore, who barely won the popular vote and who, if you look on a county-by-county map, carried approximately 15% of the geographic area of the U.S.? If so, he probably won't be very effective, because he will have an uphill battle pushing his more liberal agenda through a hostile Congress. That will be Clyde's fault, too.

Whatever happens, Clyde's to blame. If he had gone to sleep on his back, Al Gore would be president-elect. Had he slept on his belly, there would be no question it's Bush.

What's Clyde have to say about it?

He is in seclusion under our bed and hasn't issued a statement, though I can tell he feels badly about the Constitutional crisis into which he has plunged us all. He hasn't been able to finish his Mighty Dog since the day after the election. And he's so depressed he's been sleeping 23 hours a day, always on his back or stomach, never on his side. That was a fluke, as fluky as the strange events that converged November 7th in Florida.

Privately, however, he told me the lesson he has learned and will never forget.

Perhaps it's not always smart to let sleeping dogs lie. Especially if they're recommending Pat Buchanan.

I slept with Patsy Ramsey

Last week in fact.

I've gotten high with Farrah Fawcett, Kathie Lee Gifford and Linda Evans.

I am the brother David Spade's mother won't tell him about.

I was O.J.'s lover.

And you thought I lived a life as boring as yours.

I majored in journalism in college, but went into advertising instead. But I've never lost my fascination with the news business.

If I could have any job in journalism, I wouldn't want Tom Brokaw's. Nor would I want to be editor of *The New York Times.*

I'd want to write headlines for the *National Enquirer, Star, Globe* or one of the other supermarket tabloids. It's the perfect combination of advertising, in which you need to be creative to capture readers' attention quickly, and journalism.

Plus, you get to sit around and laugh your head off all day.

I never buy these titillating rags but always flip through them in line at Stop & Shop. (And don't you act holier-than-thou, you do too. That's why they're all dog-eared.)

My interest, I assure you, is purely intellectual. Specifically, I always try to find the one morsel of truth in every story—and there has to be one, otherwise the paper would be sued for libel—that enables the headline writer to make whatever preposterous claim about whatever celebrity the rag features on its cover.

For example, a recent *Enquirer* headline trumpeted, "Matt Lauer's Wild Night With Drag Queens."

Turns out his wife, as a joke, arranged for a "trio of transsexuals" to perform lap dances for Matt and pal Bryant Gumbel one evening at a Manhattan restaurant. Matt's wife and Bryant's girlfriend were on hand for the hilarity. An odd gift for sure, but it's not like Matt was out cruising gay bars.

"How Britney Spears Escaped From JonBenet Nightmare" screamed a headline in a recent *Globe*. Was the princess of pop in the basement of the Ramseys' Boulder home that fateful Christmas night? Can she tell us who the murderer was?

Nope. When she was six, her mother took her to a kids' beauty pageant, like the ones in which my bedmate Patsy used to enter JonBenet. But she "was appalled at what I saw," Britney's mom writes. "All those mothers telling their daughters that appearance was the most important thing in the world."

I think the real story the reporter missed is that the singer's mother can't spell "Brittany."

A recent *Examiner* revealed, "J. Edgar Hoover Was Black." This news flash comes from a book by Mille McGhee, an African-American who remembers her grandfather in 1957 told her about her great-great-grandmother who had eight children with her white master. "And he said one of their sons, Ivy Hoover, had a son named J. Edgar."

The same issue has a cover story, "Shocking Claim: Mr. Ed Was a Zebra," about a rumor posted on a web site. " 'Hardy-har-har,' " laughs Alan Young, the 81-year-old human star of the show, " 'That's a good one.' " The story, then, is nothing more than a report of a rumor. A tabloid can spin a cover story out of a rumor, so long as it acknowledges it as a rumor.

By the way, if you're wondering how I can say I slept with Patsy Ramsey, it's simple.

Last week I was reading John and Patsy Ramsey's book, "The

Death of Innocence," which has their photo on the cover. I dozed off with the book on my chest. Though I didn't physically sleep with Patsy per se, I did sleep with her likeness which is, of course, hers and hers alone. So in a sense I did sleep with Patsy Ramsey. It's all a matter of creative interpretation. And, under the libel laws, I can get away with it. I just did in fact.

I once flew from LAX to JFK aboard a jet on which Farrah Fawcett was a passenger. I rode up in an elevator with Kathie Lee. A former co-worker, Linda Evans, and I shared a ski lift during a company outing.

David Spade and I really are brothers. I was a member of Sigma Alpha Epsilon at the University of Missouri. My alumni magazine reports he was an SAE at Arizona State. Under the fraternity's bylaws, we're brothers. His mother doesn't know me from Adam.

As for me being O.J.'s lover? Well, I used to love O.J., but it's too acidic for my 48-year-old digestive system. So I don't drink it any more. You could say I dumped O.J.

While most tabloids have their own reporters who are well-versed in libel law and know just how far they can stretch facts without being sued, a few accept stories from "stringers"—freelance writers. I'm working on my first freelance piece now, thanks to a tip from my college roommate, Ed, who lives in Arkansas.

Ed knows a guy who, in the early '60s, was a Boy Scout in Hot Springs. Bill Clinton was a member of his troop. This guy told Ed, who told me, about a cookout the Hot Springs troop held in which the scouts were roasting hot dogs on sticks over an open fire. Some of the more rambunctious boys started sword-fighting with their sticks, causing a few of the hot dogs to fall off into the open flames. This guy isn't sure if Clinton's was among them.

And that, my friends, is a story that, if I play my cards right, could sell a gazillion copies of some tabloid and earn me enough to quit my day job and go to work for the *Enquirer.*

I'm gonna headline it, "Clinton's wiener may have fallen off."

What? You think our spinmeister-in-chief—a man history will remember for his creative interpretation of certain facts—will find that offensive?

If he does, I have two words for him.

Sue me.

What do women talk about?

It's no secret what men talk about when they get together. Men talk about sports, cars, the stock market, and, of course, women—but only in a positive way.

"Boy, just look at that pretty dress!" Or, "Doesn't she look fit today!"

But what do women talk about?

When a man asks his woman what she talks about with her girlfriends, we always get the same lame answer. "Oh, girl stuff, you wouldn't understand."

Every man wonders, because we're paranoid our women are telling their girlfriends intimate secrets about us that will send them into gales of laughter the next time they run into us at Stop & Shop.

The truth is, we'll never know what women talk about when we're not around.

We'll just have to assume our wives and girlfriends, when they get together, talk about the same important issues we see them discussing in TV commercials—namely, how they avoid bearing our children, how they stay fresh even after they've finished the Iron Man Triathlon and, of course, how we men continue try to ruin their lives, even from the grave.

These slice-of-life commercials—mankind's only view into what women discuss when they're together—drive me nuts.

Take the commercial for birth control pills that's running on every channel these days.

Three attractive young women, each representing a different ethnic group (the Bimbos, Bimbettes and Bimbinos), have gathered for lunch and, to their glee, discover they all not only use the same method of contraception but—miracle of miracles—the same brand! Why, one of them just happens to be carrying her plastic pillbox right now, so the rest can admire it.

Thrilled beyond belief to have discovered this common bond, they manage, in 30 seconds, to remind each other of all the benefits this particular brand affords them, including the fact that it's 99% effective—which they marvel over—and that it helps control zits which, of course, none of these babes have ever experienced.

The one percent failure rate of those pills concerns me because these three idiots definitely shouldn't reproduce themselves. Let's see, if two of them have sex 33 times over the next year and one has sex 34 times, odds are the next time we see them together they'll be attending a baby shower where they'll undoubtedly be talking about . . . hemorrhoids.

Men, have you ever once discussed with other guys what type of birth control you and your woman use? Of course you haven't, birth control is a woman's responsibility. (Just checking to see if you're still reading.)

Then there's the commercial featuring two women walking along a beach. "Can I ask you a question?" the younger woman asks. "How do you stay as fresh as an April shower, even after you've 'entertained the troops,' so to speak?"

The older woman is SO happy she asked—she's undoubtedly been hoping she would—and just happens to have in her purse a can or bottle of whatever scent she uses for this unfortunate affliction. She carries it everywhere—even to the beach—so she can "freshen up" when she feels like it.

Guys, when you're out to dinner with another couple and your woman and the other gal get up and announce, "We're going to the little girls' room to powder our noses," don't believe it. What's going on in there you don't want to know.

But there's one commercial that really drives me over the edge—the one with four senior women around a table playing bridge.

One of them is taking pleasure in informing the group she heard that another friend's husband, when he kicked the bucket—as he was probably happy to do if his wife was anything like these gossipy dames—didn't leave enough money for a decent funeral.

The others agree that would be awful if it happened to them. One confides what her Harry—who loves her SO much—has done to assure they'll have full-blown funerals complete with Cadillac hearses. He's run out and signed up with some insurance company that, for a small pittance per day, covers funeral costs. The others agree they're going to make sure their husbands sign up, too.

My question is this. If these women don't have enough money in the bank for their funerals, why are they sitting around playing cards? They look fit enough. Why aren't they working at McDonald's—which is desperately recruiting seniors to help out during the lunch hour rush—and trying to scrape together the bucks for a plot of land, headstone and coffin with a nice spray of carnations on top?

Jeez.

Ladies, you don't like this column and are going to report me to N.O.W? Don't blame me, I'm just telling it like it is. Blame the advertisers who are making you look like imbeciles.

Call or write the Association of National Advertisers and insist they portray you as you really are—as educated, modern women concerned about moist cakes, your husband's cholesterol levels, and seeing that your children ingest healthy snacks like yogurt instead of the pizzas topped with melted Snickers they're actually eating the moment your back is turned.

You are woman, make sure they hear you roar and correct these stupid misconceptions we men have about what you discuss when we're not around.

If you won't help yourselves, don't complain if we don't care enough to buy burial insurance so, while your friends are all happily playing golf in Florida or Arizona, you have to work at McDonald's to pay for our and your funerals.

And if for any reason, we go to our reward and leave you destitute, for God's sake don't go blabbing about it to your friends.

Let's just leave that our little secret, shall we?

Rainy days and Mondays always you-know-what

Last weekend the weather was crummy, the sun didn't shine once.

All day Saturday I filled in trenches in the yard—some as deep as 3 feet—dug by our beagle. She apparently hears voices calling to her from under the soil. *"Bella, Bella, we're trapped—free us!"* Our yard had begun to resemble John Wayne Gacy's.

Sunday, I drove my son to the Jersey shore where he was to spend a week with a friend. En route we ran into the worst rainstorm I've ever driven in. Cars were pulling off the Merritt Parkway onto the shoulder. The rain ended by the time we arrived in Jersey, but the Garden State Parkway was a parking lot both ways. Eleven hours down and back. Got home at 7 p.m. The day was shot.

Monday I woke and ran to the computer to check an E-bay auction. I collect art-deco Air France posters. A poster I've coveted for years—one of the rarest, for which I've searched the world—had been listed for a week. I had placed a hefty bid just before I had gone to bed the night before. I was the only bidder at that point. In the middle of the night, 10 seconds before the auction ended, someone outbid me by $5.

I went into the kitchen to make coffee. No filters. And no Taster's Choice in the pantry, just Sanka. I decided to go to work early and to stop for coffee.

I hopped in the shower. No soap.

It was another gray day, with rain predicted. Driving down Route 7 to my Norwalk office, traffic came to a halt in front of Dunkin' Donuts. A wreck ahead. After 10 minutes of not moving, I turned around and took back roads, arriving at the office 51 minutes after I left home. I could have walked faster.

There was an e-mail from a client canceling a project I had planned to work on all week.

I went to my bank to cash a $50 check. On Friday I had deposited a check for more than $1,000,000 with the same teller, who has waited on me probably 50 times in the last year. (I didn't get to keep the money; it was earmarked to pay postage for a multi-million piece mailing). Without so much as a flicker of recognition, she asked for identification.

Disgusted, I decided to spend my lunch hour at the gym, to work out the pain in my back from Saturday's yard work and the leg cramp from Sunday's 11-hour drive.

When I flashed my membership card at the front desk, the manager told me I owed two months' back dues. The dues are deducted automatically from my credit card account every month, and I remembered seeing them on the bills. After much back-and-forth, it turned out to be a computer error.

In the locker room after the workout, I was overcome by noxious fumes when removing my old sneakers. In no rush to get back to the office, I went to Bob's Store to buy a new pair. Rap music was blasting from MTV screens installed throughout the store. I couldn't hear myself think. I want soothing background music—someone like James Taylor—when I shop. But he's even older than me and now appears only on PBS specials, surrounded by children who have no clue who he is or who he was. I grow old, I grow old, I shall wear my Nikes with mold.

Despite the noise, I found four styles I liked. The store was out of my size in all of them. As I exited, the sky opened as if Niagara Falls were passing overhead.

Hungry and with a pounding headache from the "music," I ducked into the supermarket next door to buy a sandwich. I got in the express checkout line. A woman ahead of me was buying four candy bars using an ATM card that wouldn't scan properly. I waited five minutes, then changed lines. My cashier ran out of register tape.

It was pouring even harder now. I ate my sandwich under the canopy and, after 10 minutes, ran for my car. I had parked it at the far corner of the lot, where it was less likely to get dinged by shopping carts. I got soaked to the bone. By the time I drove out of the lot, it had quit raining.

Bloomberg Radio announced the Dow Jones average was up almost 100 points.

Parking my car at the office, I saw it had been dinged after all.

I checked my stocks on the Internet. They were all down.

My phone message light was on. My wife had called. The painter had arrived to paint the shutters I had custom-ordered from a craftsman I found on the Internet. I hadn't taken them out of the boxes since they arrived. They were the wrong sizes. My shipment, I learned after five phone calls, belonged to someone else. Our shutters, apparently, were in Oregon.

I got a call from a car salesman, telling me he thought I'd look good in a BMW SUV.

The last person out of the office, I saw packages at the front desk containing work for overnight delivery to clients. Fed Ex had forgotten to pick them up. I detoured to Fed Ex in South Norwalk.

When I got home, the dog was so excited to see me she vomited dirt on the rug. She had swallowed a stomachful digging new holes that afternoon, which was easy after the rainstorm made the soil soft.

There was one letter from the IRS and another one summoning me to jury duty.

I'm not hungry. I'm not wanting for anything. Everyone I love is healthy. I know I'm blessed among men.

But blessed or not, some days it just doesn't pay to get out of bed.

37-DRYD

Aunt Evie's outhouse and the flood of '41

On a recent visit to Missouri, I drove my 87-year-old mother, Ruby, halfway across the state to Davis, the tiny town to which she and my father had moved in 1933. She hadn't been back in 20 years. Ruby said she had been thinking about Davis a lot for the last few months, as she has been writing her memoirs—which she intends to present to her children and grandchildren for Christmas—on her computer.

Because I write for a living, Ruby showed me the first draft of what she had written, and asked my opinion. I told her the truth. It was good work.

And it was clear to me as I read that, despite all the hardships she described during her 11 years in Davis, those years were the happiest of her life.

When we arrived in Davis, we found that not only had the town changed, it was gone.

Though seven or eight buildings were still standing, not a soul was living there. Apparently the flood of 1993 that devastated much of the Midwest killed Davis once and for all.

Truth be told, there wasn't much to Davis to begin with. At its peak, it had a population of only 100 or so. Ruby said that on the very day they arrived, the train tracks were being taken up by a railroad crew—hardly a good sign.

My parents were newlyweds when they moved to Davis. Like most young people caught up in the vortex of the Great Depression, they had high hopes, but no money and no prospects. My grandfather bought the store for them, and paid $500 for it.

Theirs was the only store in town, and for miles around. The newlyweds moved into a house next door, so the young wife could bring her husband meals she prepared on a wood-burning stove.

Davis didn't have electricity. Nor was there indoor plumbing, residents had to use outhouses, built behind their homes.

As we drove toward Davis, Ruby told me the story of Aunt Evie, a devout elderly woman who, one night while entertaining the minister, looked out her window to see her outhouse in flames. The minister had excused himself to use the facilities, but had decided to sneak a smoke, which he failed to properly extinguish. Evie's outhouse burned to the ground.

Shortly thereafter, during the flood of '41 that inundated the entire town, her replacement outhouse was carried away. "I don't think the good Lord intends for me to have one," Evie told people in all seriousness.

Ruby was in high spirits, and told many other stories about Davis during our two-hour drive. I had heard many of them before, but they're always entertaining.

"I want to take pictures so I can scan them into my memoirs," she announced suddenly, as we were halfway there. We pulled into a truck stop and bought a disposable camera.

I had only been to Davis once before. My parents (thank you, God) had left in 1944, years before I was born. Remembering my one visit when I was 10 or so, I knew it was unlikely there would be much to see, or that Ruby would find anyone she knew.

But neither of us had any idea the town would be gone.

Davis is nestled in valley. We arrived from the west, descending the steep hill to which Ruby said she had fled in the middle of the night with my older brother during the '41 flood. My father, she said, stayed behind to try and save the store, and was found on its roof the next day by rescuers in a rowboat. She directed me to the store.

We pulled up in front of a pile of corrugated tin and lumber that had once been the store, but which had been bulldozed sometime in the last few years, probably after the '93 flood. Next to the store where the house was supposed to be—the house in which she had lived and loved and given birth to two of her three children—there was nothing. Only the well from which she used to draw water.

"Oh my," she exclaimed, gasping for air as old people with iffy hearts do when they are startled. "It's gone. Even the sidewalk your father poured between the house and the store. It's all . . . gone."

My eyes saw a pile of rubble in the center of a weed-covered lot. But hers, I could tell, saw a store with farmers on the porch playing checkers, a strong young husband working inside it, a house with a fence, and tow-headed toddlers riding tricycles on a sidewalk.

I opened the car door, and asked if she wanted to come with me. "No," she said, softly but firmly.

I walked to the pile of rubble, hoping to find something—anything—I might take back to the car and present to her, something she would recognize. But there was nothing.

When I turned around, Ruby had gotten out of the car, and was standing on the road. Her eyes were misty, her chin was quivering.

"Are you OK?"

"I don't want any pictures after all," she said.

We drove slowly out of town, past the empty lots where she said the Baptist and Christian churches had stood and past the abandoned houses of long-deceased people she thought of as family, because they were to her, a young bride stuck in the middle of nowhere, far from home.

We crossed over a creek. "That's where I brought our bedsprings to clean the mud out of them after the flood," she said.

Ruby was quiet, and didn't look back as the car climbed the steep hill and left Davis with its vacant houses behind forever.

As soon as the town was out of sight, she was herself again, talking about the new sofa she plans to buy, how she's teaching herself Microsoft Word, and how she is looking forward to attending her granddaughter's college graduation in New York next spring, if her heart holds out.

She said she'll be sure and bring the camera, and maybe we can use it then.

As close as brothers

Most guys ask their brother to be "best man" when they get married.

My brother didn't.

And so, needless to say, I didn't humiliate my family by drinking too much liquor and proposing a drunken toast to my brother and his bride at their wedding.

I humiliated them by getting into a fistfight with the flower girl. I was ring bearer. I was five years old.

My only brother, Jerry, is 16 and a half years older than me. (Go ahead and laugh. Our parents named us Tom and Jerry, just like the cartoon. I don't know what they were thinking, either.)

Other than the fact that we have the same parents, Jerry and I have nothing in common. I always assumed the differences between us were attributable to the fact that our parents' DNA had somehow mutated between 1934, when he was conceived, and 1951, when I was.

For starters, we look nothing alike. He is 6'2" with Viking-blond hair that refuses to gray, a muscular build, and skin that never ages, even though he will be 66 in July.

I never quite cleared 6 feet, my once-brown hair is almost all white, have had to watch every bite I ever ate so I wouldn't balloon up like the Michelin man, and while I'm still in my forties (for 241 days and 13 hours, not that I'm counting), I'm already as wrinkled as a Shar-Pei dog.

Jerry pitched for his high school and college baseball teams, majored in math in college, still plays organized softball, and carries his power tools wherever he goes because he can fix anything. His idea of a perfect vacation is spending a month at the Cincinnati Reds training camp in Florida where he is right now, watching every boring pitch. His back yard, on which he lavishes hours of meticulous care, is as manicured as an English garden. In his spare time, he's tracing our genealogy, and e-mails family members excitedly whenever he discovers some ancestor's grave in South Carolina or Scotland.

I'm completely uncoordinated; can't add or subtract; wouldn't attend the World Series if it were held in my back yard, which it will never be because it's as overgrown as a Congo jungle; can't drive a nail, and see no point in tracing our family tree because they're all dead and were probably just like him anyway.

According to our mother, he takes after her father. I'm apparently a ringer for our father's father.

We both have blue eyes. That's the extent of what we have in common.

While there's no overt hostility between us, for most of our lives we haven't had much to say to each other.

I don't remember living in the same household with my brother. He left for college when I was one, married and joined the army when I was five, made me an uncle when I was six.

He was raised by young parents, struggling to make a living during the Depression and WWII years. By the time I came along, circumstances had changed. I never had to make do with used bicycles, as he did. I got new ones.

My freshman year of college, when campuses nationwide were exploding in protests and "Four Dead in Ohio" was the number-one song, my brother was serving a tour of duty in Vietnam.

At Christmas 1972, when I was 21, with hair down to my shoulders, we got into a shouting match over the war. I said things I still regret. He probably does, too.

When I was two years out of college, just starting my advertising career, he retired after 20 years as an Army Intelligence officer, then embarked upon a second career doing something with computers, I never understood what.

Growing up, I always envied guys who had brothers with whom they could play games, ride bikes, build treehouses and soapbox derby racecars.

The happiest moment of my life was the day my wife gave birth to our second child. We had known intuitively that our first child was a boy. We assumed our second would be a girl.

The day our second child was born, three years after the first one, and I saw he was a boy, I was on top of the world. These Dryden brothers, unlike the previous generation, would be close. They would be best buds who would play together, laugh together, complete each other's sentences. And when they grew up, they would be best man at each other's weddings.

Little could I imagine they would be as different from one another as Cain and Abel, whose behavior toward one another theirs closely resembles.

My sons are nothing alike. One is lean, fair and red-headed. The other is muscular, with olive skin and brown hair. One is a founding member of the philosophy club at Wilton High School. The other is on the wrestling team. One is extremely vocal. The other is the silent type.

Though they were raised together, and even had many of the same teachers at Driscoll School, they share no interests I've ever been able to discern other than baseball. One is a Mets fan. The other loves the Yankees.

It's clear to me the only traits they share are the same parents, same last name and . . . blue eyes.

I've been thinking about how I could possibly be the father

of two sons who apparently have nothing in common and have decided there's only one answer that makes sense.

It's genetic.

My life-to-be as a dog

If there is such a thing as reincarnation, I know what I want to be when I come back. A dog.

Not just any dog, a Dryden dog. It's the cushiest job on earth.

I'm a dog person (as opposed to a "cat" person. Cat lovers generally listen to Pavarotti during dinner and read Proust for fun).

My wife and kids love dogs as much as I do.

In our 24 years of marriage, we've had a total of seven dogs—two at a time, sometimes three—even when we lived in closet-sized high-rise apartments in Chicago and Manhattan.

Though most of our friends seem to favor dignified golden retrievers or yellow labs, we, for some reason, always wind up with small neurotic dogs. Over the years, we've shared our homes with a dachshund-corgi mix, two long-haired dachshunds, two beagles, a smooth dachshund and—the one non-neurotic exception—an extremely laid-back terrier-mixed mongrel from Aruba

Right now we're down to two—Bella, a sad-eyed beagle I found at the Westport ASPCA, and Clyde, an upbeat dachshund with a perpetually wagging tail and a voice as shrill as Owen Meany's. I want to get one more, but my wife says two are enough. (She'll come around, she always does.)

Whereas all our friends' dogs can fetch, play dead, roll over and probably do algebra, the dogs we have (and have had) are as dumb as stones, despite the fact that each has a certificate from obedience schools attesting to his or her brilliance.

Two were even sent away to boarding school for six weeks, where they must have learned which fork to use during dinner courses, because they're sure didn't learn to come, sit or stay. It cost me more to educate those dogs than to attend a state university for four years in the early '70s. I'm convinced the school's owners took the dogs to a kennel and, with the money we paid, took an around-the-world cruise.

Dumb though they may be, our dogs have lived like royalty.

When we were young and living in New York in the late '70s, we took a trip to Ireland. To save money, we stayed in bed and breakfasts for $25 a night. We were paying that much for each of the dogs back in Manhattan in a luxury doggie hotel, where they were probably ordering room service.

Now that we're suburbanites, the dogs stay in a local luxury kennel when we travel, where they check in to doggie "condos" and, for all I know, golf on doggie golf courses and play water polo in doggie swimming pools.

When we're home, they spend most of their time dead to the world, snoring loudly as they lounge on our best upholstered furniture, punctuated by 50 trips a day to and from the yard, where they're confined by an invisible fence.

Our beagle finds the fence particularly frustrating, since she wants to chase deer and other animals which, of course, don't wear electronic collars like she does.

One sadistic rabbit has figured out the dog can't cross the invisible fence. This rabbit lets Bella chase it until she has to come to a screeching halt to avoid a nasty jolt of electricity. The rabbit then stops five feet past the invisible fence shockline, and turns around, as if taunting, "You can't get me." Bella howls in frustration. Some day I'm going to turn off the power and that rabbit will be sorry.

We feed the dogs twice a day, though you wouldn't know it, because they're always hungry for more. I can't believe what dogs will eat the minute your back is turned.

Sybil, the dachshund-corgi mix, once ate an entire bowl of ham glaze—a pound of brown sugar mixed with orange juice. One Christmas, Seymour, a dachshund, ate a coffee can full of turkey grease from under the stove, and, for dessert, a pound of Godiva chocolates someone had left under the tree, with no apparent ill effects.

Dixie, a beagle, once opened the screen door to a neighbor's kitchen, and leapt up on the counter where the neighbor had left a freshly-made bowl of tuna salad. The neighbor had stepped into another room for a moment to ask her husband if he wanted a sandwich. When she returned, the tunafish was gone and Dixie was licking her lips.

Though they give us endless pleasure, the dogs are costly to maintain. Dixie had a distended kidney and required special food for 10 years, Bella has epilepsy, and takes pricey phenobarbitol tablets. Quincy, another dachshund, had surgery to remove bladder stones the vet presented to us in a little jar. I considered having them set into a ring for my wife since she owns no gemstones that costly.

Seymour once fell into a funk, refusing to eat, so we brought in a dog psychologist, who came to our home twice a week for months and pronounced him depressed. One morning at 5 a.m. the "psychologist" called from the hospital to tell us he had been mauled by a Rottweiler and wouldn't be coming for his session with Seymour that day but that perhaps we should consider giving him Prozac.

We needed it more than Seymour for being that stupid.

Dryden dogs enjoy free education, healthcare, fine hotels and all the gourmet food they can eat. They get to romp with my kids and are held and kissed by my wife 20 times a day. Best of all, they get to spend all day luxuriating in the home I have to work like a dog to pay for, without having to make mortgage payments.

That's the life for me.

Maybe next time.

Ask me. I'm happy to help.

Since I started writing this column, I've received dozens of e-mails and calls from readers, asking my advice. While I don't pretend to be an advice columnist, I'm always happy to hear from you, and to answer your questions to the best of my ability.

Q: *How can I keep deer from eating my precious ornamental shrubs?*

A: The Connecticut Bureau of Wildlife Control informs me deer are deathly afraid of coyotes, which Wilton has in abundance. So here's an idea. Each day for four weeks, place several pounds of raw sirloin around your shrubs. This will attract coyotes, who will keep the deer at bay. After a while, the deer won't even think of coming into your yard!

Q: *Should Weston be allowed to run its sewer lines through Wilton?*

A: Sure, why not? Weston allows our oversized SUVs on its roads. Seems fair.

Q: *It's summer, the kids are home and they're driving us crazy! Can you recommend a wholesome activity in which the entire family can participate?*

A: The Wilton Family Nude Recreational Swimming Association (WFNRSA) meets every Thursday at 9 p.m. during June, July and August at Merwin Meadows Pond. Leave your modesty at home, bring towels and a six-pack of soda or bag of marshmallows for the post-swim campfire.

Q: *I'm new in town and am looking for a community service organization that needs volunteers. Any recommendations?*

A: The Doubting Thomas Foundation needs you! As a volunteer, you'll spend the summer sorting through hundreds of 25-year-old unused wedding presents—avocado-green fondue pots, crepe makers and other vintage appliances—that fill the basement and attic of a Wilton home. You'll set up a tent on the town green to sell these antiques on Labor Day Weekend. All proceeds will go to the Foundation, which provides a six-month sabbatical to a deserving local columnist to be selected by a committee.

Q: *We've spent the last two years interviewing pediatricians . . . meeting with the principals of both elementary schools in town to determine which school best reflects our educational philosophy . . . and hiring a decorator for the nursery of our stretch colonial. Now we're ready to conceive our first child. But we have a concern. Once our child reaches Wilton High School, how can he or she qualify for the freshman Humanities course, for which classroom space is limited? You're a parent of high-schoolers. Any advice for us?*

A: Yes.

Q: *Seems like whenever it rains, snows or the wind blows, most Wilton homes lose power for days. How can we avoid losing power in storms?*

A: Pay the utility company to bury the power lines on your property so they can't be hit by lightening or falling tree limbs. That way, after a storm, you'll be able to luxuriate in your Jacuzzi while your neighbors are playing Abe Lincoln by candlelight.

Q: *I think it stinks that Stop & Shop designates plum parking spaces in front of the entrance for people with babies. Don't you?*

A: Absolutely! It's unfair to penalize people who practice birth control by forcing them to park near River Road, where their vehicles may be dinged by runaway shopping carts. So here's a tip. If you have a small dog, park in one of these spaces, place the animal in a Snuggli or stroller, and take it into the store with you. If people say anything, reply "he's my baby" and they'll leave you alone. If you don't have a small dog, our miniature dachshund, Clyde, will be happy to accompany you for six cans of Mighty Dog or a pound of rare roast beef from the deli department.

Q: *I never know what to expect when I open my paper. Sometimes your column makes me laugh, sometimes it takes me cry. Why is that?*

A: Because you're going through menopause.

Q: *What can I do about SUV drivers who pull up on my right when I'm trying to make a left turn, blocking my view of oncoming traffic?*

A: Here are two suggestions. A friend of mine carries a toy pistol in her glove compartment. Whenever an SUV pulls up on her right, she jumps out of her car, yells "freeze" and points it. She reports SUV drivers take off fast! Or, you can do as I do. Lay on the horn, lower your window and shout, "You self-obsessed, anti-environmental pig, how dare you think your life and your time are more valuable than mine?"

Either method should do the trick!

Q: *I'm being driven out of town by high property taxes. What can I do?*

A: Real estate has appreciated dramatically thanks to the run-up in the stock market. This being an election year, it's unlikely the market will crash until after November, when voters realize they've elected another knucklehead president. So take a page from history.

After the 1987 crash, Wilton real estate plummeted 50% in value. My advice is to sell your home now and spend part of the proceeds on an around-the-world cruise. By the time you return tanned and rested, the election will be over and the market will have most likely gone south. You'll be able to buy your home back for 50 cents on the dollar from the out-of-towners who paid $895,000 for your modest bungalow and can no longer afford the payments. Use the extra cash to pay your property taxes.

Q: *I'm terrified. All my neighbors have Lyme Disease. What can I do to protect myself and my family from this insidious disease that seems to afflict so many Wiltonites?*

A: Move to Arizona.

You are the wind beneath my wings

I always wanted to fly.

As a boy, I spent countless hours flat on my back in the yard, scanning the skies for planes flying cross-country, trying to guess where they were coming from, and where they were going.

Every Saturday morning, I tuned in faithfully to my favorite TV show, Sky King, about a rancher who flew around Arizona in his plane, "Song Bird," solving heinous crimes. The show opened with a twin-engine Cessna flying across the screen, and rolling off to the left as a voice announced, "Out of the clear blue of the western sky comes . . . *Sky King.*"

When I was 16, I signed up for flying lessons at the nearest airport, in Fulton, Missouri. Learning to fly, I quickly realized, required something I didn't have—serious money. Luckily, I was able to convince the hottest-looking girl in my class, Bobette Whanger, whose family was rich, that she should take lessons with me. That way, we could split the cost of the aircraft rental.

Alas, after our second lesson, Bobette decided her flying days were over and out. Unable to afford lessons on my own, I was grounded.

Life happened—college, career, marriage, kids—but I never gave up my dream of slipping earth's surly bonds.

Finally, last month, I signed up for flying lessons, at Danbury airport.

When I showed up for my first lesson, I was taken aback by my instructor, Rocco, who looked younger than my oldest son, a high school senior. "Can I see your pilot's license?" I asked. I wanted to make sure this kid was old enough to drive, much less fly. Turns out Rocco is older than he looks, born in 1979.

As we were waiting on the taxiway, fifth in line for take-off and with planes landing on the runway beside us every few seconds, Rocco explained that the single most important attribute a pilot must have is the ability to concentrate. "You can't let your mind wander for a nano-second," he said.

I assured him I've never had trouble concentrating. Especially when so much is at stake.

Speaking of steak, have you eaten at Porterhouse on Washington Street in South Norwalk? Phenomenal steaks. I always start with a Caesar salad. It's big enough for two, so I have the waiter put half in a doggy bag so I can have it for lunch the next day.

Finally, the control tower announced, "Cessna four-oh-one-kay, you're schmeared for Rosh Hashanah." (Lots of static in those headsets. I'm sure I'll figure out the lingo soon.) Rocco turned the plane onto the runway, pushed in the throttle and off we went.

Within seconds, we were airborne, lurching up and down violently, like the "Back To The Future" ride at Universal Studios.

I shut my eyes, and held on. Five minutes later, above the turbulence at 3000 feet, I opened my eyes, looked down and saw my own neighborhood. My house, my wife's red station wagon in the driveway.

Rocco announced I was in control, and, for the next 30 minutes, I practiced banks, climbs, descents, and learned how to adjust the trim to keep the plane level.

He even let me fly the plane back to the airport. A mile from the end of the runway, atop a high hill, Rocco pointed out a lake surrounded by million-dollar homes. Residents have complained about aircraft noise so much that pilots have to avoid flying over it. (So why did they buy houses near an airport in the first place?) Pilots have to veer to the left, then swing back to the right to line up with the runway. Rocco took control for the final approach.

About 50 feet before touchdown, we were struck by wind shear that turned our two-seater on its side, like a teeter-totter. Rocco quickly righted the plane, and once on the ground, told me it was the trickiest landing he had ever made, that we should have gone around, but were too low and too slow at that point.

I rushed to the Pizzeria Uno at Danbury Mall, and downed two stiff drinks. But, to both mine and Rocco's amazement, I returned for my second lesson a few days later.

It was hazy that day, so we stayed on the ground, learning the parts of the plane and discussing emergency procedures, like what to do when you notice your wing is on fire. "Nine times out of ten, it's faulty wiring on the navigation lights," Rocco explained.

I don't want to know what causes it the tenth time.

A minimum of 40 hours flying time is required to get my pilot's license. I'm eager to get mine, so I'm now flying twice a week. Each time, I've flown over Wilton.

I'm having the time of my life. And you, on the ground, have nothing to worry about because Rocco, with his 21-year-old lightening-fast instincts, is great. He was able to pull the plane out of the stall I had put it into over Merwin Meadows, and was downright heroic the time he seized the controls when I about to hit the steeple of the Congregational Church.

If all goes according to plan, I'll be soloing the Saturday of Memorial Day weekend. My flight plan calls for me to take off, fly over Wilton and circle back to Danbury.

It's no exaggeration when I say that you, the people of Wilton, will most definitely be the wind beneath my wings that day. I just hope they're not on fire.

So keep your eyes open. If you see a little Cessna circling high above Wilton Center, wave. If I've figured out how to flap my wings, I'll wave back.

And for God's sake . . . *duck.*

Plunged into despair

I don't ask for much.

A job to go to. Food in my belly. A roof over my head. Toilets that work.

Ah, but a man's reach should exceed his grasp, or what's a heaven for?

If you live in a home built before 1992, you probably have no idea what I'm talking about. Your toilets work as reliably as the Swiss Federal Railroads.

But if you live in one of the new stretch colonials that have popped up all over town in the last few years, or in a home in which toilets have been replaced with new models since 1992, you know exactly what I mean.

I grew up in what would be termed in Wilton an underprivileged household. We had only two toilets. Nevertheless, we were, in retrospect, blessed because both our plain white Kohler toilets functioned beautifully. When it came time to flush, you pushed the lever and—whoosh—it all went bye-bye.

Today I live in a house that has four toilets. Only one—the American Standard fixture in the kids' bathroom, installed in the early 80s when the house was built—actually works. The others are for show.

The toilet in our master bathroom—also installed when the

house was built—is a designer color no self-respecting toilet user would ever associate with natural bodily functions. Nevertheless, it matches the bidet right next to it (which, because we're not French, we've never quite figured out what that's for, so we keep it filled with water for the dogs).

This exquisitely delicate piece of porcelain sculpture was clearly created by some effete *artiste* who has never had to use a toilet. It's perhaps a foot tall, including the tank area housing the mechanism that's supposed to rise with incoming water after each flush. I say "supposed to rise" because the mechanism broke the day after we moved in. As a result, the water ran constantly, like Niagara Falls, so I had to turn off the toilet's water supply.

Seems like it should be easy to replace that mechanism, but I've called in plumbers from as far away as Greenwich, where I figure everyone has an equally upscale toilet, and none have ever been able to make it work.

"So why not buy a new one?" you ask.

Because it wouldn't work either. Trust me. Our other two toilets were installed during a remodeling project in the mid-90s. They don't work at all.

Who's to blame? Congress.

Year after year, the doo-doo gooders in Washington refuse to enact legislation restricting the sale of guns. Instead, they focus on issues they deem truly important to our life, liberty and pursuit of happiness: our toilets.

The Energy Policy and Conservation Act of 1992 outlawed 3.5-gallon tanks, tanks that held enough water to whoosh away the contents of an average toilet bowl.

In lieu of toilets that actually work, Congress required that every toilet manufactured after 1992 be designed to require no more than 1.6 gallons of water to flush. The avowed purpose of this ill-conceived legislation? To save water.

I can understand requiring people who live in moisture-challenged Phoenix or southern California, where the water has to be pumped in from Norway or some place like that, to install tiny tanks. Having to live with non-functioning toilets is a small price to pay for living where the sun shines 365 days a year.

But it doesn't make sense for those who live where there's plenty of water.

I've never worried about how much water my toilets, washing machines or dishwasher consumed. My property has its own well. The only time we ever ran out of water was when a bolt of lightening struck the pump.

All I know is that when they were first installed and I wanted to flush one of our two new toilets, I had to flush at least twice—sometimes more—to ensure no telltale signs of whatever I was doing in there remained. It probably took just as much, if not more, water to flush one of our new politically-correct model toilets than our trusty one-flush American Standard.

Half the time, no matter how many times I flushed, the new toilets simply clogged up. During the 90s, I earned enough American AAdvantage miles buying plungers and Drano with my AAdvantage Visa to take two Business-Class trips to Africa, where the outhouses always work. But eventually, it became such a pain in the body part that comes in contact with toilets to keep them running, that I turned off the water supply to those, too.

Nowadays when we have guests, we no longer serve refreshments that might necessitate a visit to the facilities.

I've been considering renting a Ryder truck and running up to Montreal some weekend soon. Enlightened Canada, you see, still allows its citizens to buy 3.5-gallon toilets. Thousands of Americans have reportedly crossed the border to purchase such toilets and bring them home. Many have been arrested by customs agents for doing just that.

President Bush, half your constituents believe you weren't honestly elected. Those who voted for you are now scared to death because they thought Cheney's heart problems were behind him.

You want America to rally behind you? Work with Congress to overturn the stupid act your father signed into law in 1992. It probably cost him his second term, outraging the citizens so much they elected Clinton, whose senator wife will undoubtedly be the next president once you and Laura have moved back to the new home you're building on your ranch in Texas . . . a home in which the 1.6 gallon toilets won't work.

As our new leader, it's not just your job to listen to constituents like me, and to act decisively.

It's your doody.

Getting our beauty rest

Not long after we married, my wife and I bought a beautiful four-poster bed. We lived in a tiny apartment, so we ordered it queen-sized. A king-size bed would have taken up our entire bedrooom. Plus, we were thin and slept intertwined, as newlyweds do. Compared to the double bed we had shared up to then, our new bed seemed as spacious as a football field.

That bed moved with us from Chicago to Manhattan to Wilton, and served us well. I would have been happy to die in it. ("Happy" is the wrong word, but you get my drift.) It was not to be.

One day last summer, my wife announced we needed a king-sized bed to put more distance between us. She said it was a necessity, she was having trouble sleeping and it was all my fault.

Whereas I can fall asleep at the drop of a hat (my son once dropped his baseball hat on the kitchen floor, causing me to doze off instantly. Unfortunately, I was driving my car on I-95 at the time), she's one of those finicky sleepers who irrationally insists that the lights and TV be turned off before she can shut her eyes. Worse yet, she wakes up easily. The sound of a flushing toilet, for instance, will wake her up, even if it's in a neighbor's home.

She claims I've started snoring (she's delusional, only middle-aged men snore), and that I thrash around during the night, as if strapped to an electric chair cranked up to full juice.

Another compelling reason for a bigger bed—and I had to agree with her—is the third occupant of it. For the last year or so, our beagle, Bella, has begun jumping onto our bed in the middle of the night, crawling under the covers and snuggling between us crossways, leaving us each approximately one square foot of room in which to maneuver.

Many nights my wife has had to get up and go into the guest room where she tosses and turns until sunrise, leaving me to wake up next to someone whose morning breath occasionally reeks of mummified squirrel carcasses.

"Fine," I said. "Go for it."

Now if it were up to me, I would have gone out and bought the first king-sized bed I saw. Not my wife. She spent her summer visiting every furniture store in the tri-state area, consulting with decorators, her girlfriends, and reading home-design magazines. She finally decided on a bed crafted out of a rare strain of mahogany cut from trees planted in years ending in "3" on some obscure Sumatran island.

We received a call last week that our new bed will be delivered in two weeks. Saturday morning, we went shopping to choose a mattress and box spring set for it. It was no fun, believe me.

My wife, you see, wants a mattress that is super-firm. When we sleep in hotels, she complains the next morning that squishy mattresses make her back ache. I, on the other hand, want a bed that's marshmallow-soft. You can't have it both ways. Something—someone—has to give.

We started at the furniture store where she had ordered our new bed.

Furniture stores kill me. The designers supposedly make the showrooms look like your home, so you'll be comfortable shopping there. Casually arranged atop the bedspread of the model of the bed we ordered were $2,000 worth of gold-brocade throw pillows, two leather-bound classics, a butler's tray with two wineglasses and a bouquet of dried roses.

When it gets to our home, it will be covered with newspapers, month-old *People* magazines and my tattered twin-sized Davy Crockett blanket I've slept with every night for 45 years (except for one month I spent in Europe in my early 20s when DREADFUL THINGS happened because I'd forgotten my lucky "bankie"). Under it all, a beagle will be snoring loudly.

We tested all three mattress/spring sets the store offered. One was hard as granite. My wife loved it. Two were pillow-soft. Perfect for me. None were acceptable.

So we went to one of those bedding chains that advertises on news radio all the time. We told the salesman we wanted a mattress that was both firm and soft. He rolled his eyes. "Doesn't everyone?"

The first mattress we saw looked as comfy as a top-of-the-line casket. It featured white quilted satin padding, brass hardware and the manufacturer's name stitched in gold thread on the front. We kicked off our shoes and lay on our sides, stomachs and backs. "Hard as a rock," my wife announced. "Soft as a feather bed," I proclaimed. "$4,495," the salesman said, drooling at the thought of a fat commission. "What else do you have?" we asked.

We spent the next hour hopping from mattress to mattress, like Goldilocks, disagreeing on each and every one in the store.

One brand, the salesman pointed out, featured "antibacterial protection." We agreed that was desirable because Bella has been known to regurgitate squirrel body parts at 4 a.m., so we decided on that brand. That narrowed our choices to 10.

Two hours later, after the salesman had waited on three other couples who made up their minds quickly and were probably sleeping in their new beds by now, we settled on an anti-bacterial "sleep system" with "12-gauge coils" and "head-to-foot helicals," whatever that means. The salesman said it had gone on sale that day, though I imagine he would have told us anything at that point to get us out of the store.

My wife says it's too soft. I say it's too hard, and too expensive, but I'll try to sleep on it anyway.

It will be here in two weeks. And I can't wait.

Shopping for it wore me out.

To my college-age niece

Dear Katy:

I'm glad you could spend the weekend with us. God, what I'd give to be 21 like you, returning to college for my senior year.

As we sat on the deck, you sipping the first glass of wine you've been served in our home, we had a discussion. It's been bothering me ever since.

You asked which schools your 17-year-old cousin—my son, who will start college next fall—had visited. I told you.

To keep the conversation going, which is often difficult between people of different generations, I then threw in an observation.

I told you that, as we've visited colleges, I've been surprised to hear admissions officers proudly announce each school's policy for ensuring diversity. Over and over I've heard the ideal class of 2005 will consist of roughly 55% females, 12% African-Americans, 10 to 20% Asian-Americans, 5% foreigners and 1% Native-Americans.

I mentioned that when I did the math, it was clear that for every 100 vacancies, only 30 or so are open for white males. Yet white males represent over 40% of the population.

You replied, "So?"

I said I found it incredible that, in this day and age, colleges would intentionally single out any group—including white males—and deny them equal opportunities for admission in the name of diversity.

You responded, "White males have oppressed society throughout history. Quotas are fair, to make up for opportunities females and other minorities were denied in the past."

I asked, "Has your white male cousin ever oppressed anyone you know of?"

You answered, "No, but white males as a group have," and abruptly changed the subject. I let it go.

But as a white male, the parent of two white males, your uncle and an American, your reply troubled me. Let me tell you why.

You're right. Women and non-whites have been denied opportunities for no reason other than their sex or color. And that was wrong.

And you're right that white males have done reprehensible things. They brought slaves from Africa. Drove Indians from land that was rightfully theirs. Ordered Japanese-Americans into prison camps during WWII. I could go on and on.

But I want to tell you today about another white man. You never knew him. He was a grocer in a small Missouri town.

Half the people in his town were African-American but they certainly didn't have the same opportunities as white citizens. The school their children attended was inferior to the white school. The roads in the "Ridge" where they lived were unpaved, unlike streets in the white part of town. Not one store on the town's block-long business district was owned by African-Americans.

They had it bad. In the early 1960s, for the first time, an African-American family moved across the Gulf, Mobile & Ohio tracks that separated the Ridge from the white side of town. They woke up their first night to find a cross burning in the yard. They hightailed it back across the tracks.

The town had two grocery stores, but African-Americans were only welcome in the store owned by this man, who always treated them exactly as he treated his white customers. Many whites wouldn't set foot in his store because of this.

He extended them credit when they were out of work; the nearby brick factory always laid off African-American employees first during slowdowns. He bailed them out of jail when they got in trouble. He lent them money when the bank wouldn't. He never hesitated to cross the tracks to deliver groceries to those too sick or old to come to the store themselves.

There were four white churches and one black church—the Second Baptist—in town. Every Saturday, the ladies of the Second Baptist Church served a dinner to raise money. No white person ever bought a plate of fried chicken, greens and black-eyed peas from them. Except him.

The man was a Methodist but, truth be told, had never cared much for the Methodist minister. As the man lay dying in 1966, one of his last acts was to ask his beloved friend, the African-American minister of the Second Baptist Church, to preach his funeral at the Methodist Church.

Now that was a big deal. Other than the cleaning lady, no African-American had ever set foot in that church. Many church members were scandalized to hear a black man would be standing in their pulpit praying for a white man's soul. Nevertheless, hundreds of people—both black and white—came out in the sleet that wintry day to show their respects for the man who had respected them equally.

It was the saddest day of my life. I was 14, and I'll never forget the last lesson my dad—your grandfather—taught me.

My point is this. There's no question many have suffered at the hands of white males. But you can't—you mustn't—lump groups of people together and judge them as one. Nor can you brand their descendants, who live in altogether different times, as "racist" or "sexist." Not all of them were, not all of them are.

In America today, white males are being discriminated against to pay for the sins of their fathers. They're not being denied opportunities altogether, as African-Americans were so unjustly denied for much of our country's history, but they're being discriminated against nevertheless, and it's wrong. And tomorrow, when society realizes white males were penalized unjustly, what group will be targeted to atone for that? White women? White college-educated women? White college-educated women named Katy, perhaps? Think about it.

And think about this. Some day you may have a son of your own. You will want him to have the same opportunities to which all Americans are entitled. Perhaps then you will understand why I believe that your grandfather—whose last affirmative action was to remind us that discrimination is wrong—would be sad his well-intentioned granddaughter is unwittingly contributing to its perpetuation.

Desiderada for the new millennium

I started college in 1969, during the height of the anti-war movement.

Millions of college students that year displayed a poster on their walls, a poem entitled *Desiderada,* supposedly found on a 17th century gravestone in an English church. It became the anthem for a generation that saw an unjust war being waged in a far-off land . . . came together to stop it . . . then, the moment the draft ended, renounced their idealism and headed off for cushy jobs in corporate America.

If you were around back then, you undoubtedly remember *Desiderada.* If not (or if you are still so addled from the substances you ingested during the '60s and '70s that you can't), here it is again. Still beautiful, but painfully out-of-date. As a public service, I've taken the liberty of updating it for the new millennium. My version appears in italics under the original. Peace, man.

Go placidly amid the noise and haste, and remember what peace there may be in silence. As far as possible, without surrender, be on good terms with all persons. Speak your truth quietly and clearly; and listen to others, even the dull and ignorant; they too have their story.

Ask your doctor if Prozac is right for you. Wear your Walkman everywhere so you can pretend you don't hear people who say "hi." Be P.C. at all times, and especially refrain from telling jokes at the water cooler, someone will surely take offense at whatever you say and sue you for mental anguish. Keep your memos short, and use bullet points—people have no attention spans. Respond to e-mails from people who outrank you; delete the rest, they're not worth reading.

Avoid loud and aggressive persons; they are vexations to the spirit. If you compare yourself with others, you may become vain and bitter; for always there will be greater and lesser persons than yourself. Enjoy your achievements as well as your plans.

Don't listen to Howard Stern, Imus or Rush Limbaugh, you've heard everything they have to say anyway. Don't compare your house to your neighbors', their garage probably holds four cars whereas your only holds two, both leased. Enjoy your Rolex, and plan now to be first in line for the next Macy's one-day sale event.

Keep interested in your own career, however humble; it is a real possession in the changing fortunes of time. Exercise caution in your business affairs; for the world is full of trickery. But let this not blind you to what virtue there is; many persons strive for high ideals; and everywhere life is full of heroism.

Keep interested in your own career, even if you suspect the pimply-faced 25-year-old MBA the boss just hired has convinced him you're redundant, which you probably are if you're old enough to remember Desiderada. Don't buy Internet stocks on margin, or believe it when you get a letter claiming the Prize Patrol has been dispatched to your neighborhood. Remember that, even as you read this, somewhere a teenager is ladling out soup to the needy in order to look better on his or her college application.

Be yourself. Especially, do not feign affection. Neither be cynical about love; for in the face of all aridity and disenchantment it is perennial as the grass. Take kindly the counsel of the years, gracefully surrendering the things of youth. Nurture strength of spirit to shield you in sudden misfortune. But do not distress yourself with imaginings. Many fears are born of fatigue and loneliness. Beyond a wholesome discipline, be gentle with yourself.

Be yourself. Especially, do not claim you've been a lifelong Yankees fan if you are doing so only to get votes. And don't be cynical about love. The divorce rate is only 50%, you might be one of the lucky ones. Collagen injections, hair transplants and eyelid surgery aren't cheap but you'll look terrific at your reunion. Keep one of those single-serve Club Cocktail martinis in the fridge, you never know when you'll need it. When the phone rings late at night and your teenager is out with his friends in his car, fear not: It's probably a telemarketer trying to sell you aluminum siding. Eat Special K, but put Half & Half on it.

You are a child of the universe, no less than the trees and the stars; you have a right to be here. And whether or not it is clear to you, no doubt the universe is unfolding as it should.

You are a child of the universe. Of course, so is Donald Trump who claims to own half of it. You have a right to be here, but remember you can't fill in wetlands, even on your own property. It's a wacky world, but hey, what else is new?

Therefore be at peace with God, whatever you conceive Him to be, and whatever your labors and aspirations, in the noisy confusion of life keep peace with your soul.

Be at peace with God, whatever you conceive Him or Her to be, and keep peace with your soul unless you drive an SUV in which case you should feel guilty for depleting the world's oil reserves and blocking others' views of oncoming traffic.

With all of its sham, drudgery and broken dreams, it is still a beautiful world. Be careful. Strive to be happy.

Hillary and Bill are still married, everyone your age seems to have made enough in the market to retire but you so you're gonna have to work until the day they carry you out of the office in a body bag, and you're never going to be a rock star or in the Olympics, but it's still a beautiful world. Buckle up for safety. If your doctor says Prozac isn't right for you, change doctors.

The Lucky Egg Club

Jane Fonda recently announced a $12.5 million gift to launch the Harvard Center on Gender and Education, which will help sociologists determine how "gender affects the development of girls and women."

Fonda's gift, she told *People* magazine, was inspired by a visit to her granddaughter's school. "They had a Thanksgiving pageant—two boys dressed like pilgrims, two girls dressed like women pilgrims. The teacher read something about the 'brave pilgrim fathers,' and the boys pretended to shoot, bang, bang. Their pilgrim wives said, 'Mercy me.' I was just floored.

"Right away, I went over to my granddaughter and said, 'You can be brave and strong, too. Don't think for a moment that you can't.' "

Good work, Jane. And now, here's an idea for the next time you're feeling philanthropic.

How about giving Harvard money to determine how nepotism in Hollywood has affected the economic well-being of thousands of talented people of both genders—actors and actresses who have to drive taxis and wait tables owing to the fact they can't get acting jobs because most of the plum roles in town are being handed out to the sons, daughters and siblings of brand-name stars?

Take a poll at any university, Jane, and I imagine you'll find drama students eager to learn how you, your brother Peter and his daughter Bridget overcame the terrible stigma of being related to Henry Fonda and somehow landed your first jobs anyway.

Now Jane, don't stereotype me as an oppressor who can't deal with self-made women like you. I freely admit you are talented. You were titillating in *Barbarella.* I kept a *Barbarella* poster on my wall during my college years. "She's a strong woman, that's why I admire her so," I told friends who commented on the costume the sexist pig director made you wear.

And you were great in *On Golden Pond.* I particularly admired your athletic physique when you did the back flip off the dock wearing that bikini. I wished then I knew more brave women like you.

But Jane, even you have to admit that the main attribute one has to possess in order to land a starring role in Hollywood these days is membership in the so-called "Lucky Sperm" club. (I agree completely, Jane. It should be called the "Lucky Egg" club. Everyone knows sperm are weak and die easily, and that eggs are tough.)

The same issue of *People* in which you were interviewed features 15 other celebrities who, like the Fondas, didn't get their jobs through *The New York Times* classifieds.

On the cover is Julia Roberts. A talented actress, I'm sure, but it didn't hurt when she went on her first casting call that her older brother, Eric, was already a movie star.

On page 6 is Marlo Thomas, who I doubt would have had her own TV show if her daddy, Danny, hadn't made sure there was room for her at his studio.

Page 8 features Gwenyth Paltrow whose father, Bruce Paltrow, directed *St. Elsewhere.* Her mother? Actress Blythe Danner. I read Gwenyth got her first job when her father and Stephen Spielberg took her to dinner. Spielberg was looking for someone to star as Wendy in *Hook.* It was a lot asking a girl to sacrifice her higher education, but Gwenyth was strong and brave. She dropped out of college, and went to work.

Sean Lennon, John and Yoko's son, appears on page 12 with his date, actress Bijou Philips, whose dad was a member of the Mamas and Papas. To the right of their picture is Natalie Cole, Nat King Cole's daughter.

A "Got Milk?" ad on page 14 shows Muhammad Ali and his boxer daughter, Laila, both wearing milk mustaches. Think she'd be in the ring if she were named Laila Smith? (And by the way, what rocket scientist ad person decided that Muhammad Ali is a good example of what drinking milk does for a body?)

Sigourney Weaver (page 36) probably didn't find it oppressive to share the last name of her father, who ran a TV network.

Donny Osmond, whose older brothers made the family famous long before he was, appears on page 42. A few pages later is Michael Jackson, whose singing brothers also blazed trails long before he set his hair ablaze during that infamous Pepsi commercial. Though they're about the same age, Donny is aging better than Michael. His nose doesn't appear to be falling off his face. Maybe Michael should drink more milk.

A 16-year-old runway model named Lauren Bush (whose grandfather and two uncles know a thing or two about nepotism) is featured on page 66, in a shot taken at an Italian fashion show. "I chose Lauren because she's the image of the new America," the designer said.

Then there's Melanie "I Can't Understand Why My Lips Are So Fat All Of A Sudden" Griffith, daughter of Tippy Hedren. Of all the legacies in *People*, she is the one who, in my opinion, would most likely be working in a Burger King if she hadn't inherited her job.

Last but not least there's Jamie Lee Curtis (daughter of Tony Curtis and Janet Lee), Ashley Judd (Naomi's daughter, Wynonna's sister) and Lisa Marie Presley, the King's princess.

And that's just one week's worth of nepotism from the pages of *People*. Future issues will no doubt feature Sheens, Baldwins, Arquettes, and dozens of other DNA-connected celebrities, all of whom are enjoying the perks of stardom while people who actually made sacrifices to study their craft are having to dice onions in the dingy kitchens of Chinese restaurants on Hollywood Boulevard in order to pay the rent.

So how about it, Jane? I'm sure struggling artists everywhere are anxious to know how, when they're reincarnated, they can come back as the children of brand names, be pictured in *People,* win Oscars and make tons of money they can give Harvard to fund P.C. causes.

Let us know when we can expect your check, OK?

My annual dose of *la joie de vivre*

All of us have our own idea of the perfect vacation spot—the place we like to return to time and again.

My idea of paradise is the Caribbean island of St. Martin, where my family spent last week's school holiday. We go every year, sometimes twice, and spend seven idyllic days following the same blissful routine—sleeping late, reading under palm trees, swimming in the bathwater-warm turquoise waters and, as the sun sets over the sea, playing Scrabble.

I'm so enamored with the place that when I die, I want my grieving family to scatter my ashes over my favorite beach (though I suppose it might diminish their pleasure on subsequent visits. *"Hey, I found a piece of really cool coral. Or is it a bone fragment from dad?"*)

St. Martin is owned by two countries. The northern half is French, the southern half is Dutch.

Though we always spend our days on the Dutch side, we spend our nights in open-air restaurants on the French side, eating like the American pigs I suspect our French waiters must call us in the kitchen when they take back our plates that look as though they've been licked clean because they usually have been.

And we enjoy watching the French people casually strolling past the restaurants as much as we like the food.

The island has been devastated by three hurricanes in the last few years. Palms have been blown over, beaches eroded, hotels destroyed. For this reason, there are not nearly as many American vacationers as there once were.

A large percentage of tourists these days are European—the majority from France—who fly in on daily Air France, AOM and Corsair flights.

The French people are what I like most about St. Martin . . . from the microscopic thongs the women wear on the beaches, to the uniformed gendarmes who patrol the streets . . . from the croissants and café au lait they order in beachside bistros as casually as Wiltonites order the #2 special at Dunkin' Donuts, to the motorized scooters on which bronzed youngsters pass you on hairpin curves, their sun-bleached hair blowing in the breeze.

I like vacationing with the French because everything about them is as different from the people with whom I deal on a daily basis as different can be. And that's what a vacation is all about—getting away from the everyday.

The most obvious difference between French and American people is our body types.

French people aren't just thin, they're skeletal, none more so than the waiters who work in the restaurants where we stuff our faces every night with dishes like *escargot, filet mignon au Roquefort* and, for dessert, *profiteroles*—puff pastries filled with ice cream and topped with hot fudge sauce. I can put on five pounds just smelling the stuff. But the waiters who serve it invariably are as thin as Gumby. I don't get it.

On the beaches, the French would be easy to spot even if they weren't thin, because the woman are almost always topless, sitting directly under the tropical sun rubbing Bain de Soleil sensuously over their exposed flesh every few minutes and smoking cigarette after cigarette.

American women, on the other hand, wear one-piece suits,

stay out of the sun as if it is to be avoided at all costs (so why didn't they stay home in the first place?) and drink bottled water while reading self-help books.

Even French dogs are different, so well-behaved their owners take them everywhere—including on vacation. One night I was fascinated to observe a French woman with teased blonde hair and pounds of make-up, wearing a leopard print micro-mini and 6-in. heels—a dead ringer for a young Brigitte Bardot—pushing two Yorkies in a baby stroller, passing restaurant after restaurant, stopping to examine menus carefully until she finally chose one, adjacent to ours.

She took the dogs out of the stroller and placed them under her chair, where they slept peacefully while their mama consumed two beers, a Caesar salad, grilled lobster, apple tart and a glass of complimentary Armagnac served by waiters with eyes bulging out of their sockets (not that I was watching every single bite she took). Our dogs would have been walking on diners' tables, lapping up their food.

Though I don't speak French, I like the romantic sound of the language. The French are fighting a losing battle to keep it pure, untainted by American influences. I read recently that the French government has outlawed use of the term "e-mail" which it considers too American and insists, instead, that its citizens refer to an e-mail message as a *"Communique d' Electronique."* Impractical, but hey—so is the Eiffel Tower.

The French present even simple things with flair. Everything in French St. Martin is artfully arranged—from store windows selling the latest fashions from Paris to the plates on which food is presented. One night my wife ordered an asparagus appetizer that was far prettier than any artwork we own, and more expensive, too. It seemed a shame to eat it.

But what I like the most about the French is how they take the time to enjoy the simple pleasures of life—their *joie de vivre.* For example, the way they linger over meals. Waiters never rush you and when, three hours after you sat down, you finally ask for the check, they seem genuinely surprised you'd want to go.

What could be more relaxing than spending time getting to know your family all over again in a tropical seaside restaurant over a beautifully-presented meal, while watching a parade of painfully thin but totally tanned people speaking the language of love pass you by?

Sitting here in my den writing this column the day after my return, I can't think of anything.

Kraft Macaroni & Cheese Dinner

For dinner tonight, I ate an entire box of Kraft Macaroni & Cheese made just the way I like it—al dente with half the milk and twice the butter the recipe on the box calls for, covered with lots of coarsely-ground fresh pepper.

It wasn't nearly as satisfying as I imagined it would be.

We just returned from taking our 14-year-old son—with whom I alone in our family share an affinity for this most banal but reassuring of comfort-food dishes, and with whom I always half-seriously argue about which of us will get the last spoonful—to summer camp.

He will be gone three weeks.

Three weeks with no ESPN blaring from the TV.

Three weeks of no arguments between him and his 17-year-old brother, who bicker about everything under the sun.

Three weeks of access to the computer I can never use because he's always playing video games.

Three weeks of having the whole box of Kraft Macaroni & Cheese Dinner to myself.

He is attending a camp for kids who will be high school freshmen this fall.

He has only been separated from us once in his life, and I could tell he was nervous. As a welcome treat, the camp was serving ice cream sundaes with hot fudge and whipped cream, but he only served himself a single scoop and didn't put a cherry on it.

We said our goodbyes suddenly, and hightailed it home.

Truth be told, it's lonely in this house tonight. Our oldest son is at the movies. Nobody was waiting to greet us but the dogs, who always welcome us home with the same simple-minded tail-wagging enthusiasm, whether we've walked to the end of the driveway to fetch the newspaper or have been gone all day.

For the first time in years, we have no summer vacation plans. My wife says this three-week lull is going to be her vacation.

She's the one who stayed up nights when the boys were sick, who got them on the bus with a good breakfast under their belts, who chauffeured them to soccer and piano lessons and the orthodonist and playdates and a hundred other places I've forgotten about if, indeed, I ever knew about them in the first place. Now that they are teenagers I'm basking in their achievements, but the credits are hers alone. She deserves a first-class cruise on the QEII, but if three weeks of peace and quiet in her own home are more to her liking, God bless her.

Control Shift.

For months, I've been thinking about writing a column about how most people I know in Wilton—and 99% of the people I know have kids my sons' age, that's how I met them in the first place—are obsessed to an unhealthy extent with their children.

Their kids are all they ever talk about.

People who have children the age of our oldest son, who will be a senior in high school, talk incessantly about college visits and proms.

People who have kids the age of our youngest drone on endlessly about what classes their children are going to take in high school, their kids' sports teams, etc.,. etc., yadda yadda, ad infinitum, ad nauseum.

I was going to say how boring it is. And, make no mistake, it *is* boring. It's pathetic that when otherwise accomplished people—educated people with beautiful homes and high-powered jobs who travel the world—get together, they have nothing more to talk about than hockey or lacrosse or homeroom assignments.

But tonight, as I sit here at this computer to which I rarely have access, I believe I understand why they're so obsessed.

For the first time since our oldest came screaming and kicking into the world 17 years ago, I'm getting a sneak preview of our life-to-be.

Fourteen months from now, God willing, we'll be taking him to college. Four years from now we'll be dropping our youngest with all his worldly possessions at some college, and we'll come home to a house that's not just temporarily but permanently devoid of children.

We're going to look at each other and wonder, "What are we now?"

We will have forgotten what we were before them, and won't know what's going to become of us without our children. What will we talk about with other people? With ourselves?

When we lived in New York years ago BC—before children—I used to pass a Second Avenue shop that displayed a t-shirt in its window that said, " If you love something, let it go. Then track it down and kill it."

The second sentence made me laugh. But the first part is true. If you love something, you have to let it go precisely because you do love it. You have to give it wings, let it fly.

That's what we did today, albeit in a small way.

But three weeks at camp is hardly letting go in the same way we'll be letting him go four years from now.

He went off today to learn new things. But when I arrived home to an empty house, I'm the one who learned the biggest lesson—that letting go is scary.

All of us blessed with healthy, intelligent children are going to have to let go of our children's place in our lives, and to fly on our own, without them.

And that is a prospect I suspect all of us—including my friends who talk endlessly about their children—find terrifying.

Our 14-year-old will be back soon. ESPN will be blaring. He'll be fighting with his brother. The sound of video games will be deafening.

And when he comes home, I'm going to try very, very hard to remember the fright I'm feeling right now . . . to bite my tongue . . . let it go . . . and savor every remaining moment.

From the (small) minds of corporate lawyers

I write ads for a living.

You may find most advertising obnoxious, but don't blame the people who create it. Blame the same people on whom society justifiably blames most of its ills: Lawyers. In this case, corporate lawyers who work for major advertisers.

They don't write the ads. Nor do they design them. Their contribution is something called "the fine print." Advertising professionals call it "mice type."

Most of these mice type-writers went to school planning on becoming the next Alan Dershowitz but, thanks to an oversupply of more talented lawyers, have been reduced to working in cubicles, red-penciling ads to make sure they cover their employers' butts in the event readers misinterpret and decide to sue.

Understandably, these Dershowitz wannabes are upset to be spending their days reviewing ads instead of arguing constitutional law before the Supreme Court. So they take out their frustrations on those of us they perceive actually enjoy our jobs—the creative people who write and design ads—by insisting on including fine-print caveats that, as often as not, contradict the purpose of the advertising, confuse readers and communicate that the advertiser isn't to be trusted.

Want legal proof? Take a look at these gems I found in magazines and newspapers on my coffee table.

In *USA Today*, Suzuki is running an ad for its XL-7 SUV, "the first affordable small SUV with a third row of seats." Now Japanese SUV manufacturers have been in the news a lot lately because some of their products have an unfortunate tendency to tip over. To avoid potential lawsuits from such victims, Suzuki's lawyers added the following. "Sports Utility Vehicles handle differently from ordinary passenger cars. Federal law cautions to avoid sharp turns and abrupt maneuvers. Even with airbags, always wear a seatbelt. For specific details, please read your owner's manual. Don't drink and drive."

Why don't they just state the obvious? "If you want a safe vehicle, for God's sake don't buy this."

Newsweek features an ad for the Dodge Grand Caravan Minivan. The copywriter (who clearly has a problem with full sentences) writes, "You can hold about anything. Thanks to Caravan's cavernous storage space. Plus a nifty new available cargo organizer with dividers for six grocery bags (1)."

The lawyer's footnote: "(1) Ask your dealer to find out when this feature will be available."

My question is this: If the feature isn't available, why did the lawyers allow Dodge to advertise it in the first place? Is it available? Is it soon to be available? Or is it just a glimmer in some designer's eye? If, in fact, Dodge can get away with advertising a feature that isn't available, it seems to me it could have just as easily promised, "You can get from New York to Bangkok in 4.5 hours with Caravan's nifty new available 85,000 hp engine with optional wings. Ask to find out when this feature will be available."

The fine print in an ad for Kinko's, a company where one takes documents to be photocopied, states, "Kinko's requires written permission from the copyright holder in order to reproduce any copyrighted work."

It's a safe bet that if Kinko's franchisees actually required such written permission, they'd be out of business quickly, and Kinko's lawyer's might have to get jobs that required them to do something useful.

A VIAGRA ad shows a man, smiling confidently. The headline: "A lot of guys have occasional erection problems. I chose not to accept mine and asked about VIAGRA."

The lawyers' contribution? "In the rare event of an erection lasting more than 4 hours, seek immediate medical help." I'm surprised they didn't insist on adding, "But don't sit in the doctor's waiting room in that condition unless you are willing to subject yourself to further humiliation."

Ever fantasize about buying one of the luxury properties advertised in *The New York Times Sunday Magazine*? Take a look at the fine print in ads for Florida properties. Lawyers for the "hanging chad" state have insisted advertisers include this clause in each: "We encourage and support an affirmative advertising and marketing program in which there are no barriers to obtaining housing because of race, color, religion, sex, handicap, familial or national origin." This from an ad for Amelia Island Plantation where homesites "start at $2.2 million."

I'm planning to sue, because, in this instance, the lawyers are being insensitive to my particular situation. While I don't face barriers because of race, color, religion, sex, etc., I don't have $2.2 million. They forgot to cover that. This has caused me much emotional duress.

A *Reader's Digest* ad for Miracle-Ear Hearing Aid Centers promises, "A hearing aid from Miracle-Ear might just help bring a little harmony back into your life." The fine print states, "Hearing aids do not restore natural hearing." Duh.

By far the most inane example of mice type I've run across lately comes from FedEx. My agency's bookkeeper logged on to Fedex.com, where he found advertising for a service called "Invoice Online" which provides instant billing information. To sign up, he had to agree to the terms. Here's what the rocket-scientist legal eagles at FedEx contributed.

"... You are not a national of Cuba, Iran, Iraq, Libya, North Korea, Sudan or Syria or a Denied Party listed on the U.S. Denied Persons List or a Special Designated National on the U.S. Treasury Department's list of Specially Designated Nationals. You further acknowledge that INVOICE ONLINE will not be used for the design or development of nuclear, chemical, biological, weapons or missile technology."

Darn. I was about to sign up expressly because I wanted to learn how to develop nuclear, chemical and biological weapons, but I suppose I can't now, because the lawyers did their job and found a clever way to forbid it.

Guess who I was going to use them on?

The gathering storm

I've been reading "Lost World of the Kalahari" by Laurens Van der Post, who, in the 1950s, spent a year searching for the Bushmen.

The Bushmen were compact desert-dwelling aborigines with yellow-mocha wrinkled skin. For thousands of years, they were the only human inhabitants of southwestern Africa, present-day Namibia. Only they, with their intuitive survival skills, could have possibly found sustenance in such a God-forsaken land.

While Bushmen spent their days stalking lion and zebra, which they would kill with poison arrows, drag home and throw on the barbie, Bushwomen spent their time gathering ostrich eggs. These they carefully hollowed out, like Easter eggs, and filled with water sucked through a reed from deep beneath the surfaces of dried-up riverbeds. They would then plug the eggshells with cork, and bury them for those inevitable days when even subterranean water supplies had dried up.

Pretty primitive stuff, but that's the way the world has operated from time immemorial. Men are hunters; women are gatherers.

And I don't have to look far to see proof of it today. This morning, in fact, I had to look no farther than our kitchen counters, which were filled with stuff my favorite gatherer has gathered.

It's Monday as I write this, and I came home from work early because we're hunkering down for the hundredth "storm of the century" in the last 10 years. (We've had four "storms of the century" this winter. Enough already.)

My wife, whenever she hears a snowy forecast, becomes as agitated as if she heard fire were about to begin raining from the sky, and, like a squirrel gathering nuts, begins running to stores, gathering anything and everything she can get her hands on. This seems more than a little irrational, given that we live in New England where it's *supposed* to snow all winter, but it's a primal instinct, she can't help herself.

This past weekend, when forecasters started talking about "up to two feet of snow," she spent the better part of both days gathering, to assure we would have everything we needed during the storm, and everything we might possibly need for months afterwards in case the snow doesn't stop until August.

She started Saturday morning by making a run to the supermarket. She came home with 20 bags of necessities for her modern-day bush family, including a box of 48 donut holes, goat cheese and brownie mix.

Sunday morning, she woke up worried she hadn't gathered enough. And so, at 11 a.m, she announced she was going out to gather more necessities, starting with gas for the station wagon.

I pointed out the tank was three-quarters full and that if we got as much snow as they were predicting, she wouldn't drive the car anyway, but she likes to keep the tank topped off, even in good weather. I, on the other hand, wait until the amber light glows on the fuel gauge, announcing the car is down to the last gallon of gas. I like to see how far I can drive before finally pulling into a gas station which I usually do only because my wife in the seat beside me is practicing the same shallow breathing technique they taught her in Lamaze class to keep from screaming.

Women are terrified of running out of gas, men like to see how far their cars can run on fumes. That's another primal difference between the species, but I don't know the scientific term for it.

Once the tank was topped off, my wife proceeded to T.J. Maxx, where she found herself shoulder-to-shoulder with dozens of other gatherers. There she gathered more necessities, including a Polar-Tec vest ("for warmth if we lose power"), a Cephalon lobster pot ("marked down twice, to $40"), and half a dozen gold-leaf picture frames. She overheard the manager remarking he had never seen such a crowd on a Sunday morning, and that he needed to open a fourth checkout line.

Her next stop was Lord & Taylor. She said she felt compelled to stop before the storm because she had received a coupon good for 20% off any sale item in the store, and didn't want the coupon to go to waste. There she gathered a sleeveless silk sweater with hot pink sequins ("Originally $80, marked down to $59.99, then to $39.98, then cut by another 50% which, with my 20% coupon, made it just $15.99."). She'll look great shoveling snow in that.

En route home, she pulled into Linens & Things, and gathered something she says is a "European bed sham," which will surely keep us warm when the sleet is beating against our windowpane and the power has been off for days.

Having worked her hands to the bone gathering, she then sought out a nail salon for a manicure, a ritual I'm sure Bushwomen always treated themselves to after a hard day of ostrich egging.

Just as the snow started falling, she ducked in the Village Market for Pop Secret microwave popcorn and Pepperidge Farm Nantucket chocolate chip cookies, vital nutrients her family needed to weather the upcoming storm.

While she was out doing her primal thing, I was doing mine. At noon Sunday, when the snow started, I went into the office to finish a proposal I had intended to complete early in the week, so I could e-mail it to a client and, if snowed in, discuss it on the phone from home.

In good weather and bad, I gotta put zebra on the table, just as my wife has to gather the other necessities we need.

Guess you could call it primal instinct on both our parts.

The Doubting Thomas summer film festival

It's exciting to see the new cinema multiplex going up in town. It would be even more exciting if there were anything I wanted to see in it. Unfortunately, most movies these days seem geared to people with the IQs of deer ticks.

I'm picky. I refuse to see any movie that stars a brand-name—anyone who's related to anyone else in Hollywood. I figure they got their jobs not because they're good but because of their family connections.

That eliminates any movie starring a Sheen or Estevez (father Martin Sheen), Julia Roberts (brother Eric), Gwenyth Paltrow (mother Blythe Danner and father Bruce Paltrow), Ben Stiller (parents Stiller & Meara), Nicholas Cage (uncle Francis Ford Coppola) and most recent Best Supporting Actress winner Angelina Jolie (father John Voight), a charming lass with multiple tattoos and cosmetically-enhanced lips that make her look like an oversized Woolworth goldfish pressed against a one-gallon aquarium.

As a result, the only movie I've seen this summer was *Perfect Storm*, to which we unfortunately returned home to a dinner of grilled swordfish. So for the rest of the summer, I plan to stay home and watch rented videos of my favorite movies. It's cheap. No lines. And you don't have to buy enough popcorn and soda to feed the Seventh Fleet.

If you haven't seen these movies, rent one. Need some company? Invite me over.

Ordinary People: This is the movie that proved, once and for all, that we WASPs are just as neurotic as everyone else. Mary Tyler Moore is an affluent housewife who sets the table days in advance, obsesses over superfluous details, has to be in total control at all times and cannot tolerate disorder in her life. In short, a flawless portrayal of my mother-in-law who watched it with me once and—I swear—remarked, "she's disturbed." It's my all-time favorite performance by an actress.

Goldfinger: OK, so it does take me back to 1964 when, as 12-year-olds, my buddy Harper and I were escorted out of the Liberty Theater in Mexico, Missouri, after the scene in which Honor Blackman karate-chopped Sean Connery, knocking him senseless. When 007 came to and asked Honor Blackman her name, and she told him, Harper yelled, "I asked what your name was, not what you have."

If you know the answer, you're laughing.

Amistad: Directed by Stephen Spielberg, this movie about a shipload of slaves was somewhat of a sleeper at the box office.

But what really blew my doors off and will yours, too (assuming you believe the North should have won the Civil War, which is probably why you have a cute little twig wreath on your door instead of a Confederate flag decal), is the anti-slavery argument delivered before the Supreme Court by John Quincy Adams, played by Anthony Hopkins. (OK, J.Q. was a brand-name just like George Dubya. However, judging from his picture in the World Book, he didn't have tattoos or collagen-injected lips).

It has to be the most eloquent soliloquy in American history. I'd never heard it before. Bet you haven't either. The hairs on your neck will stand on end.

American Beauty: Who can't identify with the characters in this 1999 film about an upwardly mobile albeit dysfunctional family? Certainly nobody in Wilton, our lives are perfect.

The best scene: When Kevin Spacey, who has exchanged his office job for one with no responsibility at the drive-thru window of a fast-food joint, encounters his wife (Annette Benning) and her lover. Spacey deserved his Oscar just for keeping a straight face.

Listen carefully to the delivery of the lines in the "bag in the wind" scene. "It was one of those days, about 15 minutes before snow began falling. The air was full of electricity, you could almost feel it." An intelligent, well-written movie, a rarity these days when morons like Adam Sandler are top box office draws.

Godfather I and II: The best performance ever by an actor. The question is, which actor? Marlon Brando in I? Al Pacino in both? Robert

DeNiro in II? Next rainy Sunday rent 'em both, watch one, break for a huge pasta dinner in-between, then watch the other. Flawless.

Saving Private Ryan: Spielberg makes lots of mindless drek, like *Jurassic Park.* Worse yet, he inexplicably hangs with Bill and Hillary. He's nevertheless my favorite director because he chooses as subjects people who stood up for right and, in so doing, changed the world—Oscar Schindler, who saved hundreds of Jews from the Nazis in *Schindler's List*; John Q. Adams in the aforementioned *Amistad* and, best of all, the GIs who landed on Omaha Beach in *Private Ryan.* The opening scene will change you forever.

Planes, Trains and Automobiles: Starring Steve Martin and John Candy, this is the story of my life when I used to travel a lot on business. If you've ever been a road warrior, you'll relate. And you'll laugh yourself silly, especially at the car rental counter scene. That's one to rewind and replay over and over. The ending drags on a bit but what comedy doesn't have its off moments?

Sunset Boulevard: William Holden is a screenwriter. Gloria Swanson is a silent movie star. She's adamant that images are more important than words. She lives, he dies, so she's clearly on to something. As an advertising writer whose clients judge his work not by his words but by the pictures that support them, I live this movie every day of my professional life. It's painful but hey, the truth hurts.

So video rental stores of Wilton, get ready. The six Wiltonites who aren't in Nantucket this month have read this column. And they're coming to take these movies away.

No talking. Turn off your cell phones. Place litter in the receptacles provided. And enjoy the show!

It's a wwwacky world

Ever wonder about the web sites listed on the packages of stuff you keep in your fridge and pantry?

I did. So, on a recent rainy Sunday, I visited some.

I started at purina.com, a site featured on a box of the Chewy Treats we keep on hand for those rare occasions our idiot dogs show some initiative.

There I took a "Breed Selector" quiz, to determine which breed of dog we should own.

I learned that, based on the qualities I value most in a dog, we should own a Bischon Frise, which earned a perfect 100% compatability score. Maybe we'll look into one when our current dogs—a dachshund (64% compatability) and beagle (42%)—pass on to that big Chuck Wagon in the sky.

A bottle of Kraft Ranch Salad Dressing directed me to kraftfoods.com, a site that seems obsessed with helping improve America's family life.

There I found tips for planning a "Family Food and Fun Night" which began with, "Select a night and time when everyone in your family is likely to be home." (Obviously not a site for rocket scientists.) Included was a menu of tasty treats to enjoy while playing board games with the family, such as Baker's ® One-Bowl

Chocolate Fudge, Philadelphia ® 7-Layer Mexican Dip, Oreo ® S'Mores and Cheesy Chili Fries.

If you really love your family, why not inject them with hypodermic needles filled with Crisco Oil instead? Seems like a faster, less insidious way to die.

Kraft also invited moms to submit their favorite tips for "delightful dinnertime activities." An astonishing number of moms, who obviously have nothing better to do, did so. Mary of Wisconsin shared this gem. "When I put something new on the table, my husband and son taste the dish, give it a score on a card and raise the card above their heads like we are at a sporting event. It's a good way to know if the dish is something I'll make again."

Here's my tip, Mary. Why don't you simply *ask* them? And consider this. Do you think your son will ever find a girl with self-esteem as low as yours, who will put up for more than a minute with the boorish behavior you find so cute? It won't be cute 20 years from now. Trust me on this Mary.

At bettycrocker.com, I was invited to "Talk To Betty," whose picture looks exactly like Laura Bush. All I had to do was type in a question and Betty promised, "You'll have your answer in a jiffy."

I asked, "Dear Betty: If you could sleep with only one of the following, who would you choose? A) Mr. Clean, B) The Gorton's Fisherman, C) Poppin' Fresh, or D) The Maytag Repairman?"

Betty e-mailed me right back. "I've been very busy working on my web site, cookbooks and new products but I always have time to correspond with friends like you." But she didn't answer my question.

At snydersofhanover.com I signed up as a member of the Pretzel Eater's Club, where I will "have the opportunity to taste-test some new product concepts for possible future inclusion in the Synder's line." My membership card is in the mail, and I can't wait to flash it next time I'm asked for identification at the bank or airline ticket counter.

I also printed out a recipe for "Pretzenality Pie" made with

Hard Sourdough Pretzels. Since I'm always in charge of Thanksgiving dessert, and haven't been able to enjoy pumpkin pie since I changed my first diaper 17 years ago, that's what we'll serve this year.

A fresh nectarine contained a sticker promoting itofruit.com. When I logged on, I entered my height and weight to calculate my body mass index, and was immediately advised to eat more fruit. I clicked on the "Fruit Action List," which told me to "buy many kinds of fruits and vegetables when you shop, so you have plenty of choices and don't run out." Wiser words were never HTML-encoded.

But my favorite web site, by far, was tasteyoulove.com, hosted by the folks at I Can't Believe It's Not Butter!® a brand that features Italian heartthrob Fabio as its spokesman. The entire site is devoted to romance.

The highlight is a weekly diary written by "Sam," a young woman who has moved to New York to "begin a new job as a writer and artist for a romance comic strip." In her first installment she writes, "I have finally called it quits with my childhood sweetheart, Eddie, after years of an off and on relationship . . . but sometimes I'm so lonely, I really want to find someone special to share my life with."

Subsequent entries introduce a series of men Sam meets in New York, whose lives all revolve around I Can't Believe It's Not Butter! ® recipes.

Listen carefully, Sam. I know you don't have a lot of experience, but these are not normal men, even for New York where the men tend to be unusual. Clearly, you've fallen in with some strange perverted cult. Get on the next Greyhound and go home to Eddie and beg him to take you back.

This site also contains a section entitled, "50 Ways to Please Your Lover." I was hoping these tips would involve creative ways to use I Can't Believe It's Not Butter! ® in lovemaking (I saw *Last Tango in Paris*, didn't you?). But, alas, they were rather tame, like "give your lover a foot massage."

There are more sites I want to visit, but I don't have time. So I'd like to ask you to visit sites sponsored by your favorite brands and let me know what you find. Maybe we can have a community Food and Fun Night where we exchange news about our favorite web sites.

I'll bring plenty of fresh fruits and vegetables. You bring the Philadelphia ® 7-Layer Mexican Dip to dunk 'em in.

It'll be wwwild.

"Please hold for Doubting Thomas"

From *USA Today:*

> *A Greek executive running late for a flight to Brussels called in a bomb threat to delay the flight, police said. Nikita Kotiadis was sentenced to seven months in jail. Police said he asked his secretary to call Axon Airlines. He then told an airline agent that there was a bomb aboard. He hoped the ploy would delay the flight until he arrived. But, instead of just dialing the airline, the secretary identified Kotiadis by name before patching him through.*

Don't get me wrong, there's nothing funny about a bomb threat. On the other hand, three of my all-time favorite business stories involve Greeks, secretaries and bomb threats. I couldn't make these up if I tried.

As regular readers know, I'm in advertising. My former business partner often communicated with me by handwritten notes, even though his office was adjacent to mine.

One day he was reading *Advertising Age* and saw a photo featuring the president of a rival agency. This other agency guy was accepting a coveted industry award for a campaign his agency had developed for a fast-food chain, a campaign that featured the Teenage Mutant Ninja Turtles. We had recommended a year before that one of our clients, another fast-food chain, use the Turtles in their campaign, but our client had rejected the idea.

My partner tore out the page and attached a handwritten note to it, which he placed in his "out" basket. "We told those idiots at (our client company) to run with the Turtles a year ago and we should have won that award, not (competitive agency name)."

My partner's longtime secretary would have known to take the article and note from his "out" box and place it in my "in" box. She, however, had quit and a new, over-eager assistant had just begun. She typed up the note as a letter on letterhead to the man shown in the picture, complete with "Dear Mr. (Name)" as a salutation, signed my partner's name, and sent it.

My partner didn't know about it for two weeks, until he found a copy of the letter in his file. He tried to call the recipient to apologize, but couldn't get through.

Another classic story involves a former client, a defunct airline.

A New Yorker touring Greece died suddenly, and his coffin was placed in the cargo hold of the airline's daily flight to JFK. Take-off was delayed six hours due to a part that had to be replaced. Airline officials called the funeral home in Brooklyn, where the family was gathered for the wake, to notify them the guest of honor would miss the party.

Almost halfway across the Atlantic, the airline received a bomb threat. The jet turned around and put down at Shannon, Ireland, where passengers were evacuated. Explosive-sniffing dogs were brought in to go through the plane inch by inch. This took eight hours, so the airline put the passengers up at local hotels. Finally, the only thing left to inspect was the coffin. Under Irish law, only a funeral director can open a sealed coffin. The airline had to contact 20 Irish funeral directors until it found one willing to open the lid without fear of it going ka-boom. No bomb was found.

The next morning, the plane took off. An hour out of Shannon, a passenger suffered chest pains, so the pilot landed in Iceland . . . where the part that had been installed the previous day failed. Iceland being the middle of nowhere, no spare part was available. The airline had to arrange to have a new part placed on that night's Icelandic Airlines flight from JFK to Reykjavik . . . and had to put the passengers up for a second night.

All this time the funeral director was calling the airline every few hours, asking where the body was, because he had a funeral home filled with flowers, but no corpse.

The third day, the plane took off once again. By the time it arrived, JFK was fogged in. The plane had to be diverted to Boston . . . where the part failed yet again. The airline sent another plane to ferry the passengers to JFK, and transferred their luggage to the new aircraft. But workers forgot to check the cargo hold in which the coffin had been stashed.

From Boston, the jet flew to the airline's maintenance facility in the Midwest . . . where, by the time it arrived, officials realized the coffin was still aboard.

It gets worse. En route back to JFK, the coffin had to "change" planes. At the connecting airport, it was mis-tagged and sent to Houston.

A week after his death, the grieving family finally got their loved one back, who had probably seen more of the world dead than alive.

When I started my career in the mid-'70s, women executives in advertising were a fairly rare commodity, and nobody had ever heard of personal computers. All correspondence was hand-typed on IBM Selectric typewriters.

An agency I worked for had just hired its first woman account executive, an exotic-looking Greek named Sophia Dolmades (not her real name, but close). Sophia thought she was hot stuff, and especially enjoyed lording her title over her secretary, Rita.

One day she made Rita type a letter five times, not because Rita had made mistakes but because Sophia had changed her mind about using certain words. Each time, Rita typed the closing, "Sophia Dolmades, Account Executive."

The fifth time Rita submitted the letter, Sophia signed it. But she didn't look carefully at the closing. Rita had typed "Sophia Dolmades" as usual. But she hadn't typed "Account Executive" underneath. She had split "Account" into two words (one an article), and omitted a "C" and an "O" from the second word.

Rita, by the way, is now a top advertising executive, in charge of the global operations of her company.

Sophia never progressed beyond account executive and the last I heard of her, was working as a secretary in her native Greece.